A JOURNEY LIKE NO OTHER

Restored by Grace

Mae Dixon

Copyright © 2019 Mae Dixon.

All rights reserved. No part of this book may be used or reproduced by any means, graphic, electronic, or mechanical, including photocopying, recording, taping or by any information storage retrieval system without the written permission of the author except in the case of brief quotations embodied in critical articles and reviews.

LifeRich Publishing is a registered trademark of The Reader's Digest Association, Inc.

LifeRich Publishing books may be ordered through booksellers or by contacting:

LifeRich Publishing
1663 Liberty Drive
Bloomington, IN 47403
www.liferichpublishing.com
1 (888) 238-8637

Because of the dynamic nature of the Internet, any web addresses or links contained in this book may have changed since publication and may no longer be valid. The views expressed in this work are solely those of the author and do not necessarily reflect the views of the publisher, and the publisher hereby disclaims any responsibility for them.

Any people depicted in stock imagery provided by Getty Images are models, and such images are being used for illustrative purposes only. Certain stock imagery © Getty Images.

Scripture taken from the King James Version of the Bible.

Scripture quotations taken from The Holy Bible, New International Version® NIV® Copyright © 1973 1978 1984 2011 by Biblica, Inc. TM. Used by permission. All rights reserved worldwide.

Scripture taken from the New King James Version®. Copyright © 1982 by Thomas Nelson. Used by permission. All rights reserved.

ISBN: 978-1-4897-2496-0 (sc)
ISBN: 978-1-4897-2497-7 (e)

Print information available on the last page.

LifeRich Publishing rev. date: 10/09/2019

Endorsements

The Grace Story: A Journey Like no Other is an uplifting book for anyone who is struggling with low self-esteem, anger, bitterness or pain.

Mae has translated what she learned from her own struggles into practical tools for overcoming the pitfalls we all encounter as we strive to grow whole and become who God intended us to be.

Kathleen Vestal Logan, MS, MA,
Author of Women's Wisdom: Pass It On!

As someone who has worked many years in the media, there is not much that I have not heard or seen. Mae shares her own personal struggle with us in her new book, The Grace Story - A Journey Like no Other. She also shares lots of anecdotes as it relates to living a grace-filled life. You can feel the love and strong desire to help others throughout this gem. You will want to share it with everyone you know who has been challenged by domestic violence, it is an excellent read for both the perpetrator and the survivor. There is nothing that cannot be overcome with grace and Mae makes it real so that one can't help but want more and more.

Linda Moorer, AKA Sonshine
Motivational Speaker
Radio Host & -Program Director Magic 106.1

This book touched me in a special way. As a survivor of abuse as a child and adult, I've found the journey to healing to be more complex and time consuming than I anticipated. I often find myself having difficulties navigating unknown territory. This book touched on deep complexities that we sometimes don't think about or address while giving us positive actionable steps to overcome. Thank you for sharing this necessary memoir, I feel inspired, encouraged and equipped to take intentional steps to live the life God intended me to!

Shafonte' L. Dixon, Officer
A Will & Way, Inc.

Dedication

This book is dedicated to my mom, Missouri Shumake, now deceased, but is still a source of strength and validation for me;

Georgena Sanchez, my surrogate mom and friend who believed in me when A Will & Way, Inc. was just an idea and has remained my source of support in every step of this journey.

And to every woman, man, boy and girl who has suffered some form of domestic violence, may you know it is not the end, but rather it's a part of the story that you are obviously living to tell. While it may not look like it now you are a Survivor.

Foreword

When I think about grace, I think of receiving something I don't deserve. Where would we be without grace? Most likely, we'd be lost in a web of waywardness with absolutely no idea how to be set free. Many may feel caught in a wayward web right now – a web created by unwise decisions and choices made against sound counseling or better judgment. What we often fail to notice is the mighty hand of God in and on our life regardless of our circumstances, so out of desperation, frustration, or maybe a sense of urgency, the need to make hasty decisions arises. Because of this, we find ourselves letting go of God's unchanging hand and walking away from our foundation of faith; thus, the need to be restored.

Although God's path may seem like a detour from the paths, we have created for ourselves (in our carnal mind), we must remember God has a plan for our seemingly crooked path. Obstacles, struggles, heartache, betrayal, and other difficulties are strategically placed for our growth, our good, and His glory. We never know what a new day may bring, yet as Believers we have the assurance that He is with us. There is no need to doubt the future when we are Christ connected. A disconnect or even a loose connection may lead to a faulty walk – another need to be restored.

Mae Dixon is no stranger to a crooked path made straight. Being restored (repaired, renovated) in Christ after a childhood of unmerited misfortunes has led to her unexpected immerse in ministry. Ms. Dixon not only speaks and writes of restoration, but she is also a conduit for restoration to countless men, women, and children by offering hope, love, and giving of self. "Restored by Grace - A Journey Like No Other" is proof of her unwavering faith. If you are reading this, know it is not by happenstance, but by divine intervention…by grace. Allow yourself to follow the path shared within these pages with confidence knowing they are Spirit-led and gifted by God's grace.

"And of His fullness we have all received, and grace for grace." John 1:16

LaVender Shedrick Williams, Author, Blogger

Preface

The African Proverb, "UBUNTU" says, "I am what I am because of who you are".

This proverb speaks my sentiment in this book. Stories are told in many ways, verbally, visually, audibly and literally and with every telling something is either added or deleted to express the emotions, ideology and or perspective of the one telling the story at that time.

Restored by Grace – A Journey Like No Other, is a compilation of my own personal experiences and tools which I have learned from childhood to senior adulthood to bring me to this place of peace that I enjoy today. Each of us have our own journey, our own stories of which no one can fully appreciate because they have not lived it. Therefore, we all demonstrate our unique characteristics, our idiosyncrasies to the world forgetting that while we may be different, we're all still the same in the universe.

Some parts of this book you will resonate with in a mighty way while others may not apply to you directly. I encourage you to pay attention anyway. If you're reading this your journey is still in an active state and since there are no coincidences… that very passage may be more valuable to your future or that of a loved one. Or, it may cause you to reflect and gain an understanding of a past incident.

For 15 years I have written a monthly newsletter which included most, if not all this information and over the years there have been hundreds, if not thousands of comments from readers declaring the benefits of having read and applied them. As a survivor of domestic violence, my self-esteem was extremely low, and were it not for books like this that I could read in private, and learn that I was not alone in my struggles; there are people who actually care; resources are readily available to accommodate my needs, and all I had to do was to reach out and trust that a process was already in place to help me to step out of the shadows of shame, guilt, fear and lack. This book will do that for you. Read it, share it and keep it close for reference as you become transformed into the person you were meant to be.

Acknowledgements

My gratitude extends to a huge tribe of wonderful,
loving and supportive people.
To my family, especially my sons, Calvin and
Demetrius and friends who have stood
in the gap for me So many times, and still
stand with me as I try to live my own
Purpose of helping to empower others in word and deed.

To the men and women who have read the many articles I've written
over the years for A Will & Way, Inc. and encouraged me to continue
for all these years. This includes the board
members, Georgena H. Sanchez,
Carolyn Jones, Karen Bonner, Carolyn Nero,
Donna Bennett, MD, Teresa Lott,
Shirley Bell, Marcia Priller, Karen Cudd,
Alfreda Shumake, Robert Allen, P.A.,
Mary Alice Brown, Niebra Washington Collins,
P.A., Kathy Strader; program leaders,
Annie Patterson, LaTanya Graphenreed, Delores
Ross, Jake Wood; service teams,
Jesse Wren, Joyce Bennett, Jim Bell, Thomas Rowe,
Charles Sylvester, Darren Lusane,

The Pensacola Bay Area Women's Council
of Realtors and volunteers.

To the Escambia County Sheriff(s), Ron
McNesby and David Morgan,
their staff at CBD, Joseph Stanberry, Sr. and the Interfaith
Jail Ministries, Inc., the women and men who were incarcerated
at CBD and who participated in the programs, Woman to Woman
and Men Talk programs. Jerome Chisholm,
Principal and our Teen Mentoring
group at Escambia Charter School

Special Program funding supporters – The Studer Foundation,
The Sansing Foundation, Sharon Kerrigan,
P.A., Margaret Stopp, P.A.,
Glory to God Ministries, Inc., Shirley Lewis
Brown, Mr. & Mrs. Richard
Appleyard, Mr. & Mrs. William Houdashelt, Mr. & Mrs. Mike French
Mr. & Mrs. Elbert Jones

To the many mentors and fellow authors who are quoted
and are featured herein.

To those from whom I have shared quotes and instructions
here and in the classroom over the years whose names I've missed;
To all who assisted with the proofreading, editing and
collaborating to bring this work to life.
Thank you so very much.

"For all have sinned and fall short of the glory
of God, being justified as a gift by
His grace through the redemption that is in Christ Jesus."
Romans 3:23-24 (KJV)

"Stop and think: Upon believing in Jesus Christ's
substituitionary death and bodily resurrection,
the once-lost sinner is instantly unconditionally, and
permanently "declared 100% righteous."
Anything less and we are not righteous….. we're almost righteous."
- Charles R. Swindoll (The Finishing Touch)

Contents

Chapter 1: Relationships: The Celebration of Life and Family 1

1. Relationships Are Important and Necessary 3
2. Family Relationships- Release Yourself from Family Karma 5
3. Friendship Provides Spiritual Inspiration 7
4. Friendship is Like a Unicorn 8
5. Parenting 10
   a. Children Learn What They Live 10
   b. Children are a Gift from Heaven 10
6. Fatherhood 12
   a. Fatherhood is Not Just a Word 12
   b. Father's Day is Everyday 13
   c. The Heart of a Father 14
   d. When a Man Becomes a Dad that's a Good Thing 15
7. Motherhood 16
   a. A Wise Woman 16
   b. A Mother's Love is Never - Ending 16
   c. Becoming A Mother 17
   d. What My Mama Told Me 18
8. Teen Chat 20
   a. A Wish Come True 20
   b. Feeling Fed Up with Life? 21
   c. High School Preparedness is Important to Your Success 22

    d. Domestic Violence Awareness 25
    e. Stay Woke 26
    f. Stand in the Face of Fear 27
    g. Go After Your More 28
9. The Dynamics of the American Family 29
    a. Where Do You Rank in The Human Race? 29
    b. All Lives Matter 30
    c. Things That I Believe 32
10. What is your LOVE Language? 34
11. The Celebration of Life and Family 36

Chapter 2: Health & Wellness: A Shift is Going On 37

1. Let's Get to The Root of the Issue 39
2. A Shift is Taking Place 41
3. Who am I? 43
4. What is Mental Health 44
5. The 10 Benefits Of Hugging 47
6. Escape from Reality 49
7. Let the Children Come 51
8. The Price of a Soul 53
9. Domestic Violence 55
    a. Know the Facts 55
    b. Depression is a Treatable Condition 59
    c. 7 Tips on How You Can Show Some Self Love 60
10. Reaching a Plateau of Comfortability 62
11. It Is All Vanity 64

Chapter 3: Forgiveness 65

1. Did You Know? Unresolved Anger is Killing Us 67
2. Anger Creates Holes in Our Heart 69
3. Don't Let the Deeds of Others Cause You to Lose Your Place in Eternity 71

4. We Can't Go Back...73
5. His Resurrection Our Forgiveness......................................75

Chapter 4: Restoration – The Cost To Be Free...........77

1. What Does it Mean to be Free, Really? 79
2. Manipulation of the Mind 81
3. Are You Willing to Be Guided?..83
4. Small Compromises Can Lead to Devastating Consequences....85
5. Just Look the Other Way 87
6. The Bridge Goes Both Ways..89
7. Love is in the Air 90
8. It's A New Season 91
9. A Letter from Our Mother (in spirit) 93
10. The Light of My Father...95

Chapter 5: Peace 97

1. When Was the Last Time….?..99
2. Favor is Not Fair 101
3. Resolve to Evolve..103
4. Who Are You Following? 105
5. Where Are You Resting 107

Chapter 6: Hope: To be Restored by Grace and Love: A Thirst that Water Can't Fill........ 109

1. A Little Help Goes A Long Way 111
2. Let's Continue to Build the Road.....................................112
3. Count it All Joy...114
4. You Can Change Your Mind..115
5. Reconnecting – What Was Old is New Again 117
6. Who's Loving You?...119

7. Focus on Who You Love 121
8. A Thirst that Water Can't Fill 123

Chapter 7: Purpose: Do Something 125

1. Reflections 128
2. Do Something 130
3. Make the Most of this Season of Repositioning 132
4. Are you a Fire Origin Species? 134
5. My Life Is Not My Own 136

Chapter 8: Grace: I Feel Love from You 137

1. I'm Thankful Because 139
2. The Sufficiency of Grace 140
3. Reflections of Gratitude 142

Chapter 9: Mission Fulfilled 145

CHAPTER 1

Relationships: The Celebration of Life and Family

Relationships Are Important and Necessary

For many years I steered clear of building relationships because I was afraid of being hurt again. I had been hurt by family members and so-called friends so many times before that my heart just couldn't take another disappointment, physical or verbal attack. As my children became older I, a single parent by now, realized that I could no longer live unto myself; I realized that there were many things that they needed that I was unable to give them such as good and positive male role models and a diverse environment that would afford them a broad perspective of life. I forced myself to reach outside of my comfort zone and to get involved in my community; in doing so I developed relationships that are still strong some 30 years later. I also lost some along the way and made many new ones.

Relationships are measured in many ways, by the way they make you feel, by what you can obtain from them, etc. You can know a good relationship when it happens because time nor distance can diminish the bond that has been established. I experienced this recently with a friend that I had not seen in a while; upon the initial greeting we picked up where we'd left off the last time we were together, catching up on our children, the latest gossip, politics and then each other - unloading our burdens, our insecurities, sharing our dreams for the future.....

We're in a season where true relationships are going to be more important than ever. In a climate where it seems that there are more takers than givers; where it's about me, mine and no more - every man being for himself. We must be careful to realize that "no man is an island", we cannot exist by ourselves. God intended that we "love ye one another" and in doing so we shall all prosper. We cannot allow fear (of a fallen economy) to separate us to the point of self-destruction. A closed fist can only receive what is in it so I encourage you as I have learned, to be fair in your dealings with others. Don't shut people out because they don't look like you or think like you. No one knows what the future holds, we're all spectators at best.

"Some people will enter your life for a reason - to meet a need, to aid you physically, spiritually or emotionally and then they are gone. Some will enter your life for a season - to bring you an experience of peace, or make you laugh; to teach you something. And some will be lifetime relationships, teaching us lifetime lessons enabling you to have a solid emotional foundation. Put what you have learned to use in other relationships and watch the world become a better place for our children and our children's children.

Family Relationships- Release Yourself from Family Karma

In an article written by Sara Wiseman, "Release Yourself from Family Karma". She talks about the many dynamics that has created so much dysfunction in families. She states, "each of us enters this lifetime through the miracle of birth--conceived by humans, pushed into the world through the body of our mother. It's said that we choose our families; that we choose our parents, siblings, cultures, even the time and place we are born into, because our souls have determined that this is where we will learn fastest on our journey of soul growth. Well chosen, or not, we are all born into family, lineage, tribe. Now, it would be lovely if the family we've landed into is brimming with nothing but love and light, a continuous feast of honey and roses. However, for many of us this is not the case. "She suggests that the seven shadows, all of which are signs of domestic violence needs to be repaired and released. They are Abuse, Addiction, Violence, Poverty, Illness, Abandonment and Betrayal. She also suggests that once you have decided to heal family karma and set clear intention to do so, you will see shifts and changes in relationships you thought would never heal; you will notice changes in others and in yourself."

Having the intention to make certain changes is the first step, it is important to note that you can't stop there. With the proper assistance mentally, this repair and release process can happen rather quickly. There are many books, audio books, videos, etc. that may be helpful if you would rather not seek the assistance of a professional. We are made up of mind, body and spirit and when any one of these components are out of sync the other components will suffer - will affect the other. We can no longer allow shame or pride which is one and the same, to rob us of enjoying our true selves.

Friendship Provides Spiritual Inspiration

"The glory of friendship is not in the outstretched hand, nor the kindly smile, nor the joy of companionship, it is the spiritual inspiration that comes to one when he discovers that someone else believes in him and is willing to trust him."
Ralph Waldo Imerson

I have been blessed to gain many friends in my lifetime, childhood friends, classroom friends, professional friends who began as colleagues, friends in the ministry and sister-friends – just 'cause.

These friends come in all shapes and sizes, varied religions and nationalities, ages and levels of maturity.

It's been these relationships that have kept me grounded. They have taught me so much and for that I am grateful. I can only hope that I have given as well as I've received. True friendship does not place demands on the other party nor does it seek to cause them harm. They listen to our tales of woe and will even cry with us. They will laugh with us and at us even if they have to apologize later.

A true friend will tell you the truth because they love you knowing that it will hurt you but trusting that you will be better for it.

Friendship is Like a Unicorn

"Friendship is like a unicorn, created from faith. Before we speak, reach out, believe in the possibility of relations with another, friendship does not exist. But when we share a meal, a joke or a walk – a piece of ourselves – we open up to friends….. one in the other person, the other person within ourselves."
(Each Day a New Beginning by Hazelden 1982)

I have so much for which to be thankful and during this season of thankfulness, one that's at the top of my list is "Friendships" I shudder to think where I might be today without a very few ride or die friends, These are friendships that have lasted beyond grade school, sickness, marriage, children, and divorce among other tragic situations. And then there are those whom I've gained through my professional career, social circles and church families.

Friends are God's gift to us and unlike family they may not and usually aren't lifetime attachments. Friends come in all colors and sizes, they may believe differently culturally or even in faith, but there is something within us that draws us to each other, that causes us to become more than mere acquaintances and have for some, result in long term love relationships and marriage.

Some very deviant forces are working in our midst to destroy the bonds of friendship in our country and the world. They must not win.

Many relationships are being tested as we try to figure out how to best combat these forces.

The languages and emotions of hate, intolerance and fear must not become the norm in our society. Our best practice for winning wars is another gift that I am thankful for, it is the Gift of Prayer; no one can control this gift for it is one that can be practiced within and without, with other like-minded people or alone. Prayer can be conveyed in words or a song.

Prayer is something that we can do and the more we do it the greater the result. To all my friends, both near and far, I ask that you will join me in praying for all that is dear to you and me. And also, the needs of our country with our friendship being at the top.

Parenting

Children Learn What They Live

When a child lives with criticism, he learns to condemn others.
When a child lives with hostility, he is easily angered and learns to fight.
When a child lives with fear, he will be apprehensive.
When a child lives with shame, he learns to feel guilty.
When a child lives with encouragement, he learns to be confident.
When a child lives with acceptance, he learns to love.
When a child lives with honesty and fairness, he learns what truth and justice are.
When a child lives in a peaceful home, he will be happy, tolerant and kind.
Inspired by Dorothy Law Nolte
and Childrenlearnwhattheylive.com

Children are a Gift from Heaven

A child is not conceived by accident, however, the act that creates the child is one that can be prevented. While the timing may be inopportune for conception, once the act is committed the results of the act becomes the responsibility of the participants.

    Why are we losing so many of our children? They are being lost to death by Black on Black and White on White crime, AIDS, suicide, drug overdose and trafficking, etc. They are also being lost due to premature parenthood, emotional breakdowns and incarceration. They're running away in search of love and a sense of belonging. Many are still in the home but have mentally moved on. It's epidemic, but there is hope.

The cycle must stop. Our future generation is self- destructing right before our eyes, and we are responsible. It's going to take the same village concept that we depended so heavily upon when we were growing up to save our children, and yes, they can be saved. Putting Prayer back in the schools is not the answer entirely, prayer in the home and in the heart is a good first step in the process. Our children are being forced (by us and society) to make too many choices without the benefit of maturity. We are trying so hard to be a part of mainstream America that we've forgotten how to be a family. We're so busy trying to keep up that we're too tired to spend quality time with our children.

Our children don't need all the stuff that we work two and three jobs to provide for them. They need our attention. The best school, designer clothing, shoes, hairstyles, designer nails, their own car, the latest technology and such will not substitute for parental guidance and supervision. Children need to have knowledge within, it will determine how well they adapt to the real world. Make an investment in their character, not their appearance.

How can a ten, twelve, fourteen or even sixteen years old successfully raise a child? They can't teach what they haven't learned. How does it affect them when they have to give up a child and live with the adult experience their body and mind has endured? We are allowing the system to dictate our children's future by allowing it to train them without guidance from us. Reflect on your childhood and evaluate how you may take those experiences and apply them with your children and grandchildren.

Let's stop being reactive and become pro-active. We must cherish these gifts (Lo, children are a heritage of the Lord: and the fruit of the womb is his reward. Psalms 127:3 KJV) or we'll continue to lose them forever. If you're thinking that because your children may be grown that this does not apply to you, think again. We are all accountable to each other and therefore the child that lives in your neighborhood or crosses your path 2 or more times a week needs you to be a part of his/her village. Don't allow fear to take away your blessing.

Fatherhood

Fatherhood is Not Just a Word

Fatherhood is not just a word., Fatherhood doesn't just happen, it's a choice made when one engages in acts that he knows has the potential to create a life.

Fatherhood is a gift of the Master Creator (God). Not all men will have this privilege, and some will, who don't want it, nor will embrace it.

Fatherhood happens when one chooses to take on the responsibility of nurturing the life of a child that he did not help to create. He may also be called Dad.

Father's Day is an acknowledgment of dads who fulfill the duties of a Father, but the true Father's Day is every day that a child of any age can feel their dad's love, support and presence in the natural or spiritual realm. Fatherhood is not a day, it's a lifestyle.

Quote

A Father demonstrates manhood by being transparent.
A Father participates in the lives of his children.
A Father loves his children enough to respect their mother.
A godly father makes sure that his children
become familiar with the Creator.

Father's Day is Everyday

As a mother who birthed two boys, I have been blessed to witness through my sons the love of a Father. Having been raised by my mom with only a few glimpses of my dad, there was a large hole in my heart and just when I was finally able to begin spending time with him, he died.

I watch my boys with their daughters and my heart just overflows with love, gratitude and amazement. A Father's influence means everything to his little girl. From daddy she learns that she's beautiful even though she's snaggle-toothed, knock kneed and a little chubby. When he looks at her with that special smile her self-esteem soars and when he speaks to her in that firm tone, she feels sufficiently chastised but loved the more.

Fatherhood is defined by relationship. It's being present for those special occasions, being financially accountable and emotionally supportive. It takes a special man to be a father and that does not always mean one having a blood relationship or a life-long tenure. It's never too late to develop the relationship of father and child. The best mentors to a child are their parents and a fatherless household robs a child of a very necessary component of their development. We salute the Fathers who live their role.

A Prayer for Fathers

Heavenly, Father, give us wisdom to walk as men of honor, to be good examples not only to our own children, but to others who are fatherless, teach us to trust you in all things, let no decision be made without inviting your input. Guide us when we waiver and meet the need when our physical ability is not enough. Help us to first be a husband before becoming a father for therein lies our blessing.

Amen

The Heart of a Father

I know very little about my own dad for he was only in my life for a very short while. I've heard many things about him both good and bad, but what I feel when I think about him is the love, the wisdom that he poured into me every time that I saw him. He was not a very affectionate man, but it was the way that he looked at me, the calm and loving sound of his voice when he spoke to me; the efforts he made to insure me that I had what I needed for my basic care. He made me feel that I was so very special.

I have sons who have daughters and I marvel at the sacrifices that they have made to be in their children's lives, to see them mature into adulthood and are still available to them. My father died many years ago and even today I yearn to know more about him, but I satisfy myself with the assurance that I had his heart, if only for a short while here on earth.

I think about the many fathers that we have encountered while serving our homeless and incarcerated population, the many tears that we've witnessed as they speak about their children - the regrets, embarrassment, loneliness and fear for their children because of their absence from their lives. There was little we could say or do aside from helping them to reconnect via letter writing, phone calls and praying with them in hopes that somehow their children would feel what they felt for them.

Life is difficult for many parents today, the advancement of technology has quietly stolen the minds and hearts of our children of all ages and as we struggle to keep up it becomes imperative that we, too, seek the heart of our Father - our heavenly Father. We are fortunate that this Father is available 24/7 to each one of us, it doesn't matter that we are male or female, young or old, rich or poor. He loves us unconditionally, He can go places where our earthly fathers can't, He sees and knows all things and loves us anyway. Imagine that if we would use our human abilities to extend this same grace to one another how much better the world would be.

When a Man Becomes a Dad that's a Good Thing

A lot of men who fathered children but left the actual parenting responsibility to the mother or another man or the government could not (in good conscience) celebrate Father's Day. Calvin, a survivor of domestic violence, a volunteer, a DAD who lives by example. He is a single parent (divorced) raising 3 of his 5 children. He is a high school graduate, military veteran, entrepreneur and homeowner.

Calvin travels frequently between states to visit with his children, he shares in their financial support and strives to maintain a good rapport with his teenage daughters.

A child who grows up without the influence of a father, a man to nurture them, they are incomplete. Just as a child, whose father is abusive will demonstrate unresolved issues which are manifested in the form of violence, larceny, addictions or mental illness. A child who grows up with love and respect from their father stand a much better chance of living a life of wholeness, healthy self- esteem and having the ability to love others.

When a man is stripped of his self-worth, his dignity, he is not alone in his plight. We're all affected and since we're all affected, we then must become part of the solution to bring about restoration; the hand of love, encouragement and resources then becomes the help.

Calvin answers the plea of many men, "**Let your hand become my help**" by demonstrating the traits of a strong & successful man, good father and friend. He relates to other men who have found themselves in bad situations, who has allowed shame, guilt and fear to back them into a corner, who's loved ones have lost confidence in them and bureaucracy have shut them out of the workforce as a result of their bad decisions,

These situations define a broken man, what are the odds that without the help of others like Calvin, you and other organizations like this these men will be given the opportunity for restoration.

We are our brother's keeper and we can make the difference between life and death, success or failure for many if we desire to do so.

Motherhood

A Wise Woman

A Wise woman is constructive and not destructive. She must learn to encourage herself if she doesn't get it elsewhere, by building her self-esteem, having confidence, and being virtuous by conforming to the ways of God and not to this world.

She's a woman who never compares herself to another and understands God is her source.

She is nurturing and directs her children in the right path and instructs them in the ways of her God.

She is careful to see to it that her actions and conversation will be an asset to her husband.

A Mother's Love is Never - Ending

One of our guardians, someone I've known for more than 20 years is a regular financial supporter of our organization when I met her, she was struggling with her daughter who was struggling with a drug addiction. Many times, she was victimized by this daughter as were others in her neighborhood. She spent many sleepless nights wondering if her child was dead or alive, maybe lying hurt in an alley someplace.

A bitter-sweet occasion brought about a grandchild, a grand-daughter. The occasion was bittersweet because now, when it seemed that she would soon be an empty nester she would have to start all over again being a mother for this child. A child, who's own mother was in no way able to care for her. In addition to taking extra care to secure her home now as she would prepare to leave for work each morning she then had to rise earlier to feed, clothe and deliver her child's child to daycare, then to school and in later years to therapy because you see, this child, her grandchild perpetuated the cycle of her mother. She has sat in the same cells - jail cells that is, as her mother; walked the same streets and alleyways and probably encountered some of the same men.

Today, the grandmother shares guardianship of her great-grandchildren with her daughter, who has won the battle over addiction and is now in a fight for her own daughter's victory. As mothers we can never let go of our children just as God never let go of us. As we commemorate another Mother's Day, I'm thinking of and praying for all mothers (young and old) who are still struggling with drug addictions, depression, are living in poverty and/or, situations of Domestic Violence. I am thankful for those mothers who pressed their way as single - parents and fathers who were both mom and dad to their children and to those who while they never birthed a child has filled the shoes for others.

Becoming A Mother

Motherhood is a gift. Every young lady who births a child will not become a mother and some mothers will have the pleasure of raising children that they did not birth.

Generally, a mother plans for the experience of motherhood. She has completed high school and maybe even college; she has cared for her body and have chosen a partner with whom to marry and father her child. For many this is the fairy tale version. The reality is mothers come from all walks of life – they are very young and without a plan, middle-aged, poor, illiterate, educated, single, diverse in race, religion and ethnicity. Motherhood is easiest when planned but is manageable otherwise with maturity and love.

Ideally, Motherhood should never be experienced until one is ready. Motherhood naturally is the result of sex between a man and a woman and often occurs between a boy and girl. In most cases it's an intentional act that should be carefully considered and reserved for marriage.

Becoming a mother forces one to grow up very quickly; it requires making sacrifices of time, energy and pleasures. It is a physical, emotional and financial responsibility. A very special bond is created between a mother and her child when all things are equal. When a child is born from one's body, no matter what happens after that you're forever changed.

A healthy relationship produces a healthy and happy child. A healthy relationship is built on love, trust and faith in something greater than oneself.

From the book "The Secret Code of Girls –
The ins and outs of being a Female" by Mae Dixon

What My Mama Told Me

My mother, having only a Fifth-grade education shared with and demonstrated some of the following quotes to me and I have found them to be true and very useful:

- Do unto others no less than what you would want them to do unto you.
- Use your head, not your back - don't rush, take time to think things through and make the best possible decision for the task at hand. Study, Learn and then apply what has been taught.
- Count the Cost - How you live today will determine your end. Live with integrity.
- A hard head makes for a soft behind - If you insist on doing things your way knowing that it's the wrong way, your latter days will be of little effect and very lonely.

- This will hurt me more than it will you but, you'll be better off for it.
- No man is an island - When we shut others out to protect who we think we are and or what we think we have we miss the true reason for being a part of humanity.

Now these quotes are not exact, but the meanings are quite clear. Life is full of imperfect beings and while some struggle continuously to turn things around it seems that fate is working against us. Having a true God-relationship gives us the strength and courage to achieve victory in this maze called life.

Teen Chat

Editorials and Articles from Newsletter for the Teens in our Youth Program

A Wish Come True

Choose your choices wisely

Have you ever heard of the Midas Touch? King Bacchus gave Midas the choice of making a wish come true. Midas' choice was that "Everything I touch will turn to gold." Now, Midas didn't choose very wisely, he chose riches over practicality. He did not think his choice through, or he would have realized that he really cheated himself.

By getting his wish for gold, he lost the benefits of all the natural resources (food, water...) And what about the people he loved, he needed to feel their embrace.

Choices should be made with wisdom and contemplation, especially ones that will shape our future. We must take the time to think things thru - weigh the pros and cons and then choose. Even if we find later that it was the wrong choice there will be consolation in knowing that we did our best.

Be careful to not put all your eggs in one basket. Choices should not be made based on our feelings; feelings can be fickle. Feelings come and go, they ebb and flow like the ocean, they're one big wave after the next. It helps when making important choices to reflect upon past experiences, you don't want to repeat bad decisions. Seek counsel, talk it through with someone you trust and pray about it. Think long-term and about the consequences.

Remember, all that glitter is not gold.

Feeling Fed Up with Life?

To focus on our own life helps us to deal better with the lives of others and their effects on us.

When hearing about the goings on within our communities and country, or what's going on next door we may get fed up with life. Being confused is an understatement! Why are people so angry, uncooperative, choosing to behave negatively when there's a way to live in and with peace?

There is no simple answer unfortunately. We, as human beings are equipped with the ability to make our own choices; those choices will inevitably affect others either negatively or positively. Our responsibility is to make sure that whatever choices we make are ones that we can live with for the long term. When we make choices selfishly and for the moment, consequences of those choices later in life may become detrimental for us and our loved ones.

The behaviors (violence, hatred, greed, selfishness) of others is to be observed but not adopted into our lifestyles. Watch "life" happen from a distance. We can see it and not become a part of it; see it and not allow it to impact the way we live our own lives. Yes, there are times when we can't escape the things that happen within our home and/or community or so it seems.

There may be times that we feel there is no one who understands or can help us in these situations. There will always be a way of escape when we seek it earnestly and it begins with being in tune with who we are and Whose we are. We are never alone, there is a Power greater than every situation, disappointment and fear. This Power lives within us and is prepared to fight every battle that comes against us - no matter how big or small. Assurance of this can be found in the Bible – "Whoever dwells in the shelter of the Most High will rest in the shadow of the Almighty". (Psalm 91 NIV) We can google this on our cell phones or tablets and read it daily to broaden our awareness and for encouragement to live victoriously.

When we can become stronger within ourselves, we are then equipped and obligated to help others who are wandering aimlessly in search of something better. It doesn't require money or things. Our love is enough - love for self and love for others.

Every day, words and actions matter.

High School Preparedness is Important to Your Success

The next few years will set the pace for the rest of your life. By now you should have already developed the basic life skills. This information is designed to propel you into adulthood and get you ready for college or your next level of learning. Do take it seriously and success will be yours.

1. **Develop Good Study Habits**

   During the high school years, homework gets more intense and grades become critical for college plans. Students planning to attend college also need to prepare for the SATs and/or ACTs. Amid all these changes, many teens are learning how to balance academics with extracurricular activities, social lives, and jobs.

   Stick to a homework and study schedule. You should have a quiet, well-lit, distraction-free place to study that's stocked with supplies. Distraction-free means no phone, TV, or websites other than homework-related resources. Ask for help when it's needed. Most teachers are available for extra help before or after school, they also might be able to recommend other resources.

2. **Go to School Ready to Learn**

A nutritious breakfast fuels you and gets you ready for the day. In general, when you eat breakfast you will have more energy and do better in school. Eat, if you can, breakfast foods that are rich in whole grains, fiber, and protein, as well as low in added sugar. If you are running late some mornings, take with you fresh fruit, nuts, yogurt, or a peanut butter and banana sandwich. Many schools provide nutritious breakfast options before the first bell.

You will also need the right amount of sleep — about 8½ to 9½ hours each night — to be alert and ready to learn all day. But early school start times — on top of schedules packed with classes, homework, extracurricular activities, and friends — mean that it's common for some to not get enough sleep. Lack of sleep is linked to decreased attentiveness, decreased short-term memory, inconsistent performance, and delayed response time. You should try to go to bed at the same time every night and wake up at the same time every morning. Turn off the phone and limit video games and TV. Napping during the day can also affect bedtimes, so it's best if teens don't nap after school.

3. **Organizational Skills**

Learning and mastering the skills of getting organized, staying focused, and seeing work through to the end will help you in just about everything you do. But this is not usually explicitly taught in high school, so you can benefit from some parental guidance with organization and time-management skills.

Parents and guardians can help you keep assignments and class information together in binders, notebooks, or folders that are organized by subject. Creating a calendar will help you recognize upcoming deadlines and plan your time accordingly. Don't forget to include non-academic commitments on the calendar, too.

When it comes to studying and homework, multitasking is a waste of time. Working in an environment free of distractions like TV and texts works best.

4. **Request Help with Studying**

Since grades really count in high school, planning for studying is crucial for success, particularly when your time is taken up with extracurricular activities. When there's a lot to study, break down tasks into smaller chunks and stick to the studying calendar schedule so you're not studying for multiple tests all in one night. Take notes in class, organize them by subject, and review them at home.

The more processes the brain uses to handle information — such as writing, reading, speaking, and listening — the more likely the information will be retained. Repeating words, re-reading passages aloud, re-writing notes, or visualizing or drawing information all help the brain retain data.

Do practice problems in math or science. If the material is beyond your abilities, seek help from a classmate or the teacher, or consider connecting with a tutor (some schools have free peer-to-peer tutoring programs).

5. **Know the Disciplinary and Bullying Policies**

All schools have rules and consequences for student behaviors. Schools usually cite disciplinary policies (sometimes called the student code of conduct) in student handbooks. The rules usually cover expectations, and consequences for not meeting the expectations, for things like student behavior, dress codes, use of electronic devices, and acceptable language.

The policies may include details about attendance, vandalism, cheating, fighting, and weapons. Many schools also have specific policies about bullying. It's helpful to know the school's definition of bullying, consequences for bullies, support for victims, and procedures for reporting bullying. Bullying via text or social media should be reported to a trusted adult and the school too.

It's also important to note that educators may call law enforcement officials to the school for serious infractions, and consequences may differ based on students' ages.

6. **Take Attendance Seriously**

You should take a sick day if you have a fever, are nauseated, vomiting, or have diarrhea. Otherwise, it's important that you arrive at school on time every day, because having to catch up with class work, projects, tests, and homework can be stressful and interfere with learning.

7. **Make Time to Talk About School with Your Parents**

Make efforts to talk with your parents or guardians every day, so he, she or they know what goes on at school and with you. They are the major investors in your future and your success and while they may be busy trying to make a home and financially provide for you doesn't mean that they are not interested in your daily life. If you don't feel comfortable talking about a certain situation, write a note or a letter. Keep the lines of communication open.

Sources: Kid's Health and Kathryn Hoffses, PhD

Domestic Violence Awareness

What do you think of when you hear this term "Domestic Violence"? Does anyone in you know come to mind? Have you been a victim of domestic violence?

1 in 3 females and 1 in 4 males have been victims of [some form, including bullying] physical violence by someone they know intimately (a friend, family member, etc.) within their lifetime.

You can Speak Out and Take Action to protect yourself and others by doing the following:

C- Cultivate a respectful attitude toward everyone in your school and all members in your family. Avoid behaviors that demean or control girls and women.

C- When you are angry with your friend, girlfriend, boyfriend, sister, brother, or parent, respond without hurting or humiliating them. Try to use a non-violent, respectful response to resolving conflicts in your family and relationships. Call a domestic violence, teen dating violence or child abuse prevention program for help if you continue to hurt friends or members of your family.

C- If you have a friend or know of a family member who is afraid of her or his partner or who is being hurt, refer them to the 24-hour toll-free National Domestic Violence Hotline at 1-800-799-SAFE (7233). Or if appropriate, to the National Dating Abuse Helpline at 1-866-331-9474, via online chat at http://www.loveisrespect.org/get-help/get-help or by texting "loveis" to 77054

If you have been personally violated in any way and you have not been able to release the fear, anger or shame that it has caused, you are not alone. There is help for you. Using the contacts above or by simply dialing 211 on your cell phone you can speak to someone anonymously and get the help needed to heal physically, mentally and emotionally. The restoration of our power begins when we begin to tell our story.

Stay Woke

A beautiful young girl - 12 years old went missing in the community and was later found dead. She made some wrong choices and lost her life as a result. This is happening more and more now that Human Trafficking is more prevalent in our country and abroad. Below are some steps to keep you, your siblings and friends safe:

A Yoruba proverb says, "After we fry the fat, we see what is left." What I've learned in retrospect is that we can save ourselves a lot of pain, regret and disappointment if we do some of the following actions now:

1. Begin within, take quiet time alone - listen with your heart

2. Trust your head, follow your first thought
3. Don't be fooled by appearances - all that glitters, is not gold
4. Be willing to be wrong - only God knows everything
5. Be flexible - for if you won't bend, you'll break
6. Do the best you can where you are with what you have
7. Be prepared - focus, study, plan and then act
8. Help somebody else
9. achieve the impossible - don't take the easy way out
10. When in doubt, pray.

Stand in the Face of Fear

When it seems that every other day there is something tragic happening within our schools and communities and the country it becomes easy for us to become fearful and want to retreat within or strike out as a means of self-protection. We must not let the enemy win. The enemy is usually someone on the outside but sometimes we become the enemy when we fail to deal with unresolved issues that may occur as a result of a personal violation, self- hatred, bullying, anger against a parent, sibling, friend or fellow classmate.

We cannot run away from these issues and therefore must seek assistance in dealing with them; we must stand in the face of fear - call it by its name and then begin to deal with it as best we can. Everyone encounters some fear in their own life and some tend to handle it better than others. When we are strong enough to share with someone we trust, our fears are less likely to cause us to take actions that may be harmful to ourselves or others.

Today, seek ways to deal both positively and safely with any issue that causes you stress, anger, fear or uncertainty. If you don't have a mentor- someone you trust with your most private thoughts, find one - it can be a teacher, pastor, parent, relative, your doctor, nurse, a friend's mother, neighbor or fellow classmate.

As we pay tribute to fallen students, teachers and friends across the country I also pray for you.

Go After Your More

What is that you might ask, "Your More"? Well I'm glad you asked. Your More is that thing that we were all born for; our purpose; that something that stays in our mind and in our heart; it keeps bringing us back to center when we go to the left or right.

Do you know that your path was predestined and that while you will have the power to choose detours along the way, you cannot escape your destiny?

You can make it easy or you can make it difficult, but the day will come when we all will have to reckon with ourselves and our God.

I hope you will go after your More with a determination like no other. The sooner you achieve your More, the better you will feel about yourself and the life that you will create for you and others.

Your More is the Purpose of your existence. You will know it when you find it. It's that one thing that brings you the most joy, it is a part of you. For some it is music, writing, dancing, being a good listener; being present for others; caring for the sick, elderly or mentally ill, a sport, art, working on cars; working with children; teaching, preaching. It is always something that you do to benefit mankind.

The Dynamics of the American Family

Where Do You Rank in The Human Race?

Who coined the words "minority" and "majority" as it relates to Human Beings? As a member of The Human Race (black, white, yellow, brown, pink, Indian, Mexican, African, European, Asian, etc.), we are all connected by blood to each other and quite frankly, we just can't get any closer than that.

Many of us allow ourselves to be identified by certain "labels" and as a result the whole of us suffer an identity crisis and the consequences thereof today. We may feel deprived socially and economically, we may feel that our financial/material wealth forces us or entitles us to live in isolation from those who are less fortunate or that people who don't look like us are inferior; not worthy of respect. We may feel challenged to spend beyond our means to, "fit in" or commit criminal acts simply to survive. We are fearful of many things and as a result, in order to make the most of this life (mentally, physically, culturally) we must begin to acknowledge our fears, learn why they exist and methods for eradicating them.

Healing is available to those of us who choose to live peacefully within this human race as equals. There is no majority nor minority, there is only you and me and we are one - derived from the same Source and no matter how much we try to create a divide, when all is said and done, we shall all return to the same earth from which we came.

We are of great value to one another, not one of us can exist independently of the other. Our diverse gifts and talents, emotional and physical strengths are a necessary source of survival. The rich can't be rich without the poor and the poor demonstrates the most basic elements of faith, and it's that faith, in whatever disguise that you dress it that sustains us all.

This season of our lives affords us another opportunity to make things right with each other and the universe. I don't know about you, but I refuse to allow fear, hate, anger and unforgiveness to rule in my life. My goal is to love unconditionally, to change those things within me that I can and give all others -in prayer to my Source, The Father, Son and Holy Spirit.

What about you? Are you bringing into this season things (emotions, beliefs, actions) that should have been left in the latter? If you answered yes, I encourage you to let them go.

All Lives Matter

Domestic Violence does not discriminate, men abuse women, women abuse men, siblings abuse each other, mom abuses dad and the children and vice versa. The political giants abuse the poor citizens; Senior citizens are victimized by their own children, on the streets and in the workforce.

People with disabilities catch it from all sides; Many who once lived large lives and due to some misfortune or their own bad judgement fell beneath their privileges and become subject to same or worse perils as other impoverished people. It's a vicious cycle and will only grow worse until we began to peel away the layers of bureaucracy and deal with the root of the issue which consist of affordable medical and mental health care, an improved educational system and financial relief for those living with less than their basic needs being met. There is no one or simple solution but it begins with the tried and true principle which is to "treat others as you desire to be treated".

Now, if you are someone who places a low value on your own self then it would be difficult for you to see most others much differently, and this is where the problem lies. It generally will have very little to do with money and the possession of it. Most rich people have lived their entire lives in a state of poverty mentally, emotionally, and spiritually and its proven by the number of poor people we have in our society. A person having high values and a healthy self-esteem will want others to prosper right along with them and will "share the wealth" to insure it happens. They will not feel threatened to the point that they would need to hoard everything for themselves and their circle of influence. It would make sense that as they assist in bringing others up with them their wealth would increase and so it goes into perpetuity. This is what will restore our country to its reputation of being "The land of the free and the home of the brave". Currently we have a situation where FEAR has a foothold on our leaders and that fear is falling into and is filling every cavity of our society and is causing us to make decisions that will haunt us throughout our lifetime.

The movements that have garnered so much attention recently, and rightfully so such as the #MeToo, Black Lives Matter, White Lives Matter, Police Matter, Children Matter, Race Matters all have one thing in common - Domestic Violence. Something happened and it happened enough times to earn a name, the one that needs to stick is "All Lives Matter" and then let it be so.

Recently there has been an outcry from some men who has now been empowered by the "MeToo movement to share their stories of abuse first sexually and now are talking about the physical abuse that they endure at the hands of women and their fear of retaliation - if only to defend themselves, from law enforcement and society. The reality is that hurt people hurt people. A large percentage if not all, of both men and women who are abusive; if they're willing to admit it and, provided they haven't blocked it from memory will tell you that someone violated them sexually, mentally, emotionally or physically at an early age. It's because of a deep-rooted anger and lack of understanding about what they experienced, which makes it difficult to heal and that causes them to respond with anger so easily.

I don't have the answers. What I know for sure as a survivor of domestic violence in all of its forms is that while some form of therapy is helpful and advised to eradicate the pain, it will take a spiritual connection, one having Infinite Power (for me it is God) to remove the root of anger, bitterness and unforgiveness. To carry this burden cripples the victim and creates disharmony for them and others with whom they share a social, and especially an intimate relationship. It inevitably affects even the most patient and understanding partner. When both partners are victims it creates a very volatile situation. A Survivor who fails to achieve healing through mental health (PTSD) counseling and or spiritual healing is still a victim.

Things That I Believe

I love to learn and so I read a lot. In my reading I encounter a lot of information that pertain to most every subject. With all of what's going on in our country and even the world currently, one of the hot topics is that of "divisiveness". If you're a Facebook friend you've read my thoughts on one or more of the pages that I manage so, I hope there are no duplications here but if so, then perhaps it needed repeating.

In this space I am sharing some of my own thoughts but mostly there are the thoughts of others for which I concur/believe. I welcome your comments both pro and con for it is in understanding another's perspective that we agree to disagree peaceably and respectfully: Our world is full of variety and surprises. When we shun someone because of the way they look, we cut ourselves off from part of life. But when we respect, if not agree with the rights of others to freely express themselves we are a wonder to everyone.

You didn't pick me. I didn't pick you. You may not like me. I may not like you. But since God picked and likes us both, we are family. Sometimes, we have to look at our painful past experiences in order to prevent their reoccurrence. When we understand ourselves better, we can move beyond the past and walk towards the future with surer, safer steps. "Masks are used by just about every culture on the planet.

They keep things hidden and show only the face we want others to see. So often we put on a different face and then can no longer identify our own self. The Mask identifies the facade we hide behind." - Nathan Sawaya

We are judged by the way we treat the poor and incarcerated. All children - of our country, the world, are our future - the legacy we leave them will determine their treatment of us as we age. We are an extension of the God we serve. God, Jesus and the Holy Spirit are one, when we join in relationship with these Three, all will be well. It's not about believing the right stuff or trying to convince God of how "good" we are. It's not simply about being convinced of the value of making the world a better place. Jesus' life and teachings show us how to be and gives us the example and challenge to be a part of transforming the world for the good.

What is your LOVE Language?

We need LOVE, and when it is absent, we become depressed, angry or resentful because others may not respond to us the way we think they should. Life can be far more fulfilling when we know our own "love language" and can then recognize that of others to whom we hold dear. Gary Chapman, after much study and observation lists "The 5 Love Languages" in his book of like title.

They are **Words of Affirmation** - verbal compliments, or words of appreciation are powerful communicators of love. **Quality Time** - it isn't enough to be in the same room with someone, focused attention, quality conversation and quality activities are all very important components and are necessary to sustain all relationships.

Receiving Gifts - Gifts are visual symbols of love and are more important to some people than others. Gifts come in all shapes, sizes, colors, they may be expensive or free. To become an effective gift giver our attitude about money may have to change. Some of us have a spending orientation, we feel good when we're spending money with others in mind and as such, we will have little difficulty purchasing or making gifts for others. Some of us are "savers" and generally experience an emotional resistance to the idea of spending money as an expression of love. We are caring for our own emotional needs in the way that we handle money. What we are not doing is meeting the emotional needs of others whose love language is *receiving gifts*.

Our greatest investment would be to *invest* in the emotional love tank of those relationships that we hold dear. The gift doesn't have to be monetary it can be the gift of self. **Acts of Service** -this can be as simple as greeting someone and holding the door for them, in our homes it may be helping with the chores, on the job it could be helping someone to finish an assignment or taking out their trash; acts of service include sharing a meal with a stranger, visiting with those in nursing homes, hospitals and homeless shelters.

And finally, there is **Physical Touch** - unfortunately in this culture that we are living, some have made it difficult to do this without suspicion on the part of the receiver. For those who really need a physical touch - a hug, pat on the back or touch of the arm, fist bump or assistance for those having mobility challenges, they will receive it with love. After all, physical touch is powerful and is a way of communicating emotional love but not abuse.

The Celebration of Life and Family

As seasons come and go many of us experience a shift in our lives, for some it may be financial, health, marriage or career. Life is about change and while change can be good it can also be challenging. The key to surviving change is having a strong foundation, that strength most often is found in relationships with God and Family. God intended that we should love one another, that we should bear each other's burdens. "For if they fall, the one will lift up his fellow: but woe to him that is alone when he faileth; for he hath not another to help him up." (Ecclesiastes 4:10 (KJV)

Christmas is a time for families to come together to celebrate the gift of Christ, who came to earth to atone for our sins. It's a time to reflect on what was and then to prepare for the new - A New Life for A New Year.

There is no perfect family, sin is in all of us therefore as family we will have our ups and downs but we're still family.

The term "Family" has evolved over the years, families have evolved over the years, adoptions & multiple marriages have produced blended families, but in the sight of God we are all family, born in His image and likeness.

Let us put aside our aughts against one another, offer forgiveness to those who have offended us, forgive ourselves and put our faith in God for a future that will be filled with love and grace.

Chapter 2

Health & Wellness:
A Shift is Going On

Let's Get to The Root of the Issue

*Bishop T.D. Jakes made a statement about the woman at the well from whom Jesus requested a drink of water. Although she had a history of adultery and fornication, "Jesus looked beyond the outward manifestation of her situation and saw her real cause of pain." Immorality was the **fruit** of her problem but the "**root cause**" of her problem is a "Spirit of Discontentment!!" (John 4:1-26 NKJV)*

I could identify with this statement I, too had that "Spirit of Discontentment" as a result of being physically, sexually and mentally abused. It was only after accepting that drink of "living water". That gave me the strength to deal with those demons of self- doubt, unforgiveness and anger, that I have learned the true meaning of living in a state of joy and peace. And now that I know, I want everyone, especially other women like myself who have fallen to their lowest point, to also know that there is hope.

I am so thankful for the many systems of support. There is so much that I don't know. As a survivor of domestic Violence, I'm learning to trust again and to reach out to those who have wisdom, knowledge and experience to reach where I can't into the lives of our young and older women alike, who continually seek love and acceptance in all the wrong places and things.

Domestic Violence, and Substance Abuse and Criminal Activity have become partners in the worst way. These issues have destroyed many families and will continue to destroy our communities quietly through sexual predation, juvenile delinquency, poverty and worst, murder if we continue to look the other way.

Immorality is evil, sinful, or otherwise wrong behavior. **Immorality** is often called wickedness and is a state avoided by **good** people. (Vocabulary.com/Dictionary)

A Shift is Taking Place

Don't Be Swayed by the March Winds or the Storms to Follow.

One can't help but notice the changes that are occurring in the atmosphere;

snowstorms in California, earthquakes in Alabama, the freezing temperatures in South Florida, nor the economic shifts as a result of wars and rumors of wars.

All these incidences are worthy of note by everyone, especially the poor who will suffer the most but also, the more affluent. When the poor is devastated by even more restraints than those with which they are already accustomed, it then becomes a process of survival. The "more affluent" then must bear the infirmities of the weak (poor) without choice through increased taxes, higher prices and unfortunately theft and other criminal actions. The poor are no longer just those who live in impoverished areas of our community, they are the former "middle class", the mentally challenged, abandoned and abused children; they are our family members, our neighbors and friends.

For when a storm comes no one is exempt. One does not have to be affluent to feel the undercurrents of the storm, but all must be prepared for the storms when they come and come, they will. We can began our preparation by stocking up now on things like love, concern for others and respect for others (regardless of their perceived status in life); The storms will come in the form of more job losses, higher food & gas costs, loss of homes, senseless killing of family members, increases of substance abuse both illegal and prescribed; an increase of burglaries and theft, all of which will cause more of our much needed healthcare and educational dollars to be spent on jails and prison costs.

Is this what you planned for your future or that of your children? Can we do anything to take the wind out of these storms? Yes, we can. Now is the time to be pro-active, to speak up and speak out about injustices; to widen the lens of our view and see beyond the veil of our own circumstance; to give where it will count the most which is in the trenches - in areas where the need is greatest and not where its popular. Adopt a family or a child in need or a classroom, align yourself and/or your resources with a struggling grassroots organization that is making a difference, for while the difference may appear small to you, the benefits to the people for whom it serves are huge.

Will you be a conqueror or a mere survivor?

Who am I?

It's the question that is being asked by many today. Many of us have been programmed to feel that we lack something. We've been taught we lack good looks, that we lack intelligence. However, we are expected to look good on the outside, so we do. We hide our feelings of inadequacy.

We become indebted to an illusion, we spend enormous amounts of money on things that are temporal (cars, clothes, jewelry, homes, cosmetics, surgeries) in hopes of fitting in, of being accepted. We choose to simply survive rather than thrive.

Who I am is a unique - one of a kind jewel, I am fearfully and wonderfully made, my features may be different from the norm but that doesn't make me any less beautiful or valuable within my own society.

I come bearing gifts that are needed as part of this universe. It is not what's on the outside of me that counts for it is only a shell. Knowing who I am inwardly - mind, body and soul is. I am me and that is enough.

What is Mental Health

Mental health includes our emotional, psychological, and social well-being. It affects how we think, feel, and act. It also helps determine how we handle stress, relate to others, and make choices. Mental health is important at every stage of life, from childhood and adolescence through adulthood.

Over the course of your life, if you experience mental health problems your thinking, mood, and behavior could be affected. Many factors contribute to mental health problems, including:

- Biological factors, such as genes or brain chemistry
- Life experiences, such as trauma or abuse
- Family history of mental health problems

Mental health problems are common but help is available. People with mental health problems can get better and many recover completely.

Early Warning Signs

Not sure if you or someone you know is living with mental health problems? Experiencing one or more of the following feelings or behaviors can be an early warning sign of a problem:

- Eating or sleeping too much or too little
- Pulling away from people and usual activities

- Having low or no energy
- Feeling numb or like nothing matters
- Having unexplained aches and pains
- Feeling helpless or hopeless
- Smoking, drinking, or using drugs more than usual
- Feeling unusually confused, forgetful, on edge, angry, upset, worried, or scared
- Yelling or fighting with family and friends
- Experiencing severe mood swings that cause problems in relationships
- Having persistent thoughts and memories you can't get out of your head
- Hearing voices or believing things that are not true
- Thinking of harming yourself or others
- Inability to perform daily tasks like taking care of your kids or getting to work or school

Mental Health and Wellness

Positive mental health allows people to:

- Realize their full potential
- Cope with the stresses of life
- Work productively
- Make meaningful contributions to their communities

Ways to maintain positive mental health include:

- Getting professional help if you need it
- Connecting with others
- Staying positive
- Getting physically active
- Helping others
- Getting enough sleep
- Developing coping skills

Source: Mental Health.Gov

Mental Illness

Mental Illness is a disease that is a medical condition and is often a by-product of Domestic Violence and poverty. While we don't know how to cure mental illness for the most part, we do know that those who are mentally ill can be healed and made whole in a way that we cannot understand, but in the way that God does... Healing is about becoming awake to the fact that we are loved. Loved by God and called to be loved by our brothers and sisters in Christ. Healing is about being made whole in God's healing embrace even if we are not cured... Jesus did not promise to fix everything we encounter in this moral life, but He said to His disciples, "And remember, I am with you always, even to the end of the age. - Judith Davis (health.usnews.com)

The 10 Benefits Of Hugging

1) Hugs make us feel "happy"! When we hug another person, our bodies release oxytocin, a hormone associated with "happiness," according to scientific studies.
2) Hugs alleviate stress! Just as a good hug increases our oxytocin levels, it decreases our cortisol or "stress" levels.
3) Babies need hugs as much as water and food! According to researchers at Harvard University, hugs help promote normal levels of cortisol necessary for child development.
4) Hugs make us better students! Students who receive a supportive touch from a teacher are twice as likely to volunteer in class.
5) Hugs improve our game! Scientists at University of California, Berkley discovered that the more affectionate members of a team are with each other, the more likely they are to win.
6) A hug a day keeps the doctor away! A hug stimulates the thymus gland, which in turn regulates the production of white blood cells that keep us healthy and disease-free.
7) A hug stops the bug! Researchers at Carnegie Mellon proved that individuals who were sick and received hugs had less severe symptoms and were able to get better quicker.

8) A hugging heart is a healthy heart! Research from University of North Carolina showed that a good hug helps ease blood flow and lower cortisol levels, which in turn help lower our heart rates.
9. A hugging couple is a happy couple! Couples that experience their partners' love through physical affection share higher oxytocin levels.
10) Hugs let someone know you care without having to say a word! According to Dacher Keltner, professor of psychology at University of California, Berkeley, we can identify love from simple human touch – imagine how much love a big hug can communicate!

Escape from Reality

The thought of escaping from reality sounds like something that many of us contemplate at the beginning of a new year. Each new year recently seems to start like a whirlwind. The resolutions we make seems like a memory before the end of January. "We are addicted to the status quo and it is killing us" says Father Richard Rohr. But how do we escape that which we've come to know as the norm? How do we break old habits and create new ones? How do we even know what's real anymore? Reality is the state, condition or quality of being real or genuine, but it seems that for many, our "real" is defined by someone else's definition which means that we are not experiencing our true self.

For this reason, we find it needful to escape. To escape is the mental relief from monotony; anxiety; the act of fleeing; to get away clear; Sometimes however, in our effort to escape, we go too far to the left or to the right. This happens most often when we fail to take the time to assess the real issues that are causing our anxiety, fear or that "something that we can't seem to put a name to".

Now is a good time to get in touch with the real you/us; to remove the blinders. I recently read a quote that say's "If you want to be miserable, look within; distracted, look around; peaceful, look up!" It's ok to be different; to be unique, to have and experience your own thoughts.

You were created by an awesome Creator, who gave you a mind of your own to think independently and a heart to love unconditionally, first yourself and then others. When we choose to operate in God's strength we then, are able to navigate life with courage and certainty. Our reality is what we make it. I choose to make mine one of peace, passion and purpose. How about you?

Let the Children Come

While I was sitting in my car in front of a children's medical center. I observed the constant flow of traffic going in and out. There were mothers with their sick children of various ages; grandmothers struggling to carry much too large children for fear of losing control if she let them walk; a grandfather who struggled to carry an infant in its carrier with one hand while using the other to hold onto his handicapped daughter, who was probably the mother and then there was the grandfather holding the hands of his two granddaughters who appeared to be 2 & 3 years old while the mother followed with her infant in her arms. All bore a very sad look, some of fear and worry for their sick child, others of weariness that though they have reached the season of rest they are now back in the role of parenting or co-parenting young children. All that said, what is certain is that the children's well-being was priority number one. These were children who were physically ill, but very well cared for.

Now imagine the plight of children who are mentally ill, many who have lost their parent(s) due to death or their own battle with mental illness or abandonment. Children who have become wards of the state or who are living in dire circumstances. We're beginning to see more of these children in food lines, living under bridges, in the woods, involved in sex trafficking, being maimed and killed in drug deals gone bad, stealing for their own survival, incarcerated, and worse.

This is not a hopeless situation but, it is a serious one. We have the power to positively impact the lives of these and other children, the question is will we? In Matthew 19:14 (NKJV) Jesus instructs his disciples to "Let the little children come to Me, and do not forbid them; for of such is the kingdom of heaven." Jesus then proceeded to pray for them. Our children are suffering needlessly at an alarming rate. You may not have a dollar to spare or a room to let but you have a voice and the ability to communicate, even if only in writing your concerns and demands to all who, are in positions to effect change. Let us start by doing as Jesus did for prayer goes where we can't, and action really does speak louder than words.

The Price of a Soul

I was struggling with the message for this newsletter because there's been several pressing issues on my heart, so much so, that I could not pick just one to share with you. I'd finally settled on one issue and sat down to write when I heard Laveranus Coles, an NFL star share on TV that for three years from age 10 he had been raped by his stepfather at gunpoint. This information, although not new to me was so painful. It made me think about all the men who are locked away. They are living under bridges, and in the woods, they seem to us to be very successful businessmen, who are a little distant or totally reclusive when not in a business situation. All or most of them are very angry, easily agitated and paranoid. They're usually very careful when establishing relationships because of the "secret" that has robbed them of any possibility of intimacy in the most sacred way.

Rape and molestation affect little boys the same way or worse as it does little girls who are helpless to defend themselves. They are forced to deal with emotions that they aren't ready for. They can't share their secret with their most trusted family members. Generally, if they have siblings, they too may be victimized and together they're afraid and/or ashamed to talk about it to each other.

Our children (grand & great-grand) as they enter or return to school, daycare, pre-k, etc., many of them will be going into new environments, there's the potential that they may encounter academic challenges, there's the potential that they may encounter unsafe situations that they are ill prepared to handle. Today having so much exposure to TV, internet, radio, I-pads, video games, etc. our children need to know about the danger that could lurk inside as well as outside their homes. It is easy to miss the most obvious signs as Laveranus' mom did whose new husband was raping her son nightly (at gunpoint) while she worked a second job.

I urge you to pay attention to the young people around you, for Laveranus, it was his striking a friend at school that drew attention to his "secret", it was an attentive and caring police officer who saw something other than rage in this young man. It was in retrospect that his mom acknowledged the signs that were 'there all the time."

Our jails, juvenile centers and mental health facilities are full of people who are dealing with unresolved rage. Many children, especially those in poverty- stricken environments live in hell daily with little hope for change.. We can't change what's done but we can prevent its perpetuation. We have the power and a responsibility to lead others out of bondage, freeing their souls to live a life of joy and peace.

Sources: redskinedwizard & Burton Dewitt (New York Jets)

Domestic Violence

Know the Facts

Violence against women is a global issue, a violation of a woman's fundamental human rights and one which threatens the lives of millions of women every day, with women living in poverty often at greater risk.

Domestic violence is the willful intimidation, physical assault, battery, sexual assault, and/or other abusive behavior as part of a systematic pattern of power and control perpetrated by one intimate partner against another. It includes physical violence, sexual violence, psychological violence, and emotional abuse. The frequency and severity of domestic violence can vary dramatically; however, the one constant component of domestic violence is one partner's consistent efforts to maintain power and control over the other.

Domestic violence is an epidemic, affecting individuals in every community, regardless of age, economic status, sexual orientation, gender, race, religion, or nationality. It is often accompanied by emotionally abusive and controlling behavior that is only a fraction of a systematic pattern of dominance and control. Domestic violence can result in physical injury, psychological trauma, and in severe cases, even death. The devastating physical, emotional, and psychological consequences of domestic violence can cross generations and last a lifetime.

For anonymous, confidential help available 24/7, call the National Domestic Violence Hotline at **1-800-799-7233 (SAFE)** or **1-800-787-3224 (TTY)** now.

5 Facts Everyone Must Know About Domestic Violence

Abuse is Common

A generation ago, abuse victims were often terrified of coming forward, worried that they would appear weak or be blamed for their abuse. Thanks to the growth of the women's movement and the victim's rights movement, as well as the lobbying of millions of advocates across the globe, we now know how common domestic violence is. Indeed, some sociologists argue that gender roles, a fixation on control, and a culture of aggression have ingrained domestic violence into the American way of life. Consider:

- A woman is assaulted or beaten every nine seconds.
- 1 in 3 women—and 1 in 4 men—have been in abusive relationships, and 1 in 5 women and 1 in 7 men have faced severe physical violence.
- 20 people are abused by an intimate partner every minute, adding up to 10 million each year.
- More than 200,000 phone calls are placed to domestic violence hotlines every year.
- Intimate partner violence accounts for 15% of all violent crimes.
- The presence of guns in a home where domestic violence is a problem increases the risk of a murder by 500%.

Both Men and Women Can be Victims

Domestic violence outreach campaigns often focus on women, but both men and women can be and are victims of domestic violence.

One study found that 40% of domestic violence victims are men. Of course, the picture is a bit more complicated: While some groups have used this figure to argue that women are just as violent as men, most domestic violence directed at men is in the form of slaps and other low-level violence. Men are significantly more likely to resort to extreme violence, to use weapons, and to kill their partners.

So, while domestic violence against men does happen and is a serious problem, women remain the primary victims. But for this reason, men who have faced abuse often find themselves stigmatized and ridiculed. If someone you love says they've been the victim of domestic violence, you should believe and support them, since no gender is safe, and no amount of physical strength or emotional fortitude protects against abuse.

Abuse Victims Face a Culture of Blame

It's not just male domestic-violence survivors who find their stories disregarded. Myths about domestic violence are common, particularly among those most likely to abuse their partners. For instance, it's common to hear some people say that, if hit, they will hit back, and so women who slap their partners should expect whatever violence the partners dish back out. These thoughts support a culture of abuse and victim-blaming.

Remember these key facts, which debunk many intimate partner violence myths:

- No amount of bad behavior can induce someone to behave violently. Victims do not *cause* their abuse, even if they are unfaithful, unreasonable, or unkind.
- Responding to violence with violence is only acceptable in cases of self-defense, not to punish the perpetrator.
- No level of violence is normal or acceptable in a relationship; a person who resorts to violence once will likely do so again.
- Domestic violence harms children even when the children are not physically abused; many police departments treat domestic violence in the presence of children as a form of child abuse.

Leaving Isn't as Easy as It Seems

Domestic violence survivors are often asked why they don't leave. But consider this: How would you feel about leaving your partner? As difficult as it may be to admit, domestic violence relationships still offer their victims something, such as financial security or a relationship with a person they love. Programs designed to help victims leave, then, need to address these concerns.

Perhaps most important, though, is the fact that leaving can be dangerous. Research consistently shows that abusers are more likely to kill their victims in the two weeks after they leave than at any other time. When considered in conjunction with the fact that leaving can spark financial troubles, not to mention the pain of losing a relationship, it's easy to understand why so many survivors are hesitant to leave.

Responding to Abuse Can be Challenging

It's not easy to know what to do when someone you love is in an abusive relationship; confronting the abuser is rarely the solution.

The following steps may help:

1. Listen to and believe your loved one. Allow them to control their own lives. If your loved one does not want to leave or call the police, do not force them to.
2. Do not get involved in their fights, as doing so may endanger you. Call the police instead.
3. Offer your loved one a safe place to stay or help him or her get to a shelter.
4. Explore your loved one's reasons for staying and offer to help. If childcare or finances are a concern, for instance, try offering some financial assistance.

We can all do our part by abandoning false beliefs, embracing a culture of safety, and supporting the victims we know.

References

- Myths and facts about domestic violence. (n.d.). Retrieved from http://www.dvipiowa.org/myths-facts-about-domestic-violence/
- North, A. (2010, April 5). Domestic violence: Are women as abusive as men? Retrieved from http://jezebel.com/5509717/domestic-violence-are-women-as-abusive-as-men...
- Statistics. (n.d.). Retrieved from http://www.ncadv.org/learn/statistics
- Joel Young, M.D.,

Depression is a Treatable Condition

According to the National Screening for Mental Health Organization (2017): Depression is the leading cause of disability in the United States for ages 15-44

Depression affects more than 15 million American adults in a given year, while only half of those diagnosed with a major depressive disorder receive treatment Up to 80% who receive treatment for depression show an improvement in symptoms.

We are often encouraged by our medical providers, family, and friends to engage in screenings to identify possible health issues, such as diabetes and high blood pressure. It is just as beneficial to participate in screenings to identify mental health issues and follow up with the recommended treatment. and spreading awareness about ways to get help and that it is OK to get help will help save lives.

Pay Attention to the Children

Our children experience stress just like we do, and just like us, it manifests itself in many ways. It is important to watch your child's (or the children around you) behavior, listen to what they're saying and watch what they are doing. If they are skipping school, getting into fights, using drugs, alcohol or displaying behavioral problems while in school or withdrawing from family and friends; it's a good chance that something is wrong. When children can't talk to an adult they know, they need to and usually will reach out to someone else so take the time to make sure that they're reaching out to the right person.

7 Tips on How You Can Show Some Self Love

Take the challenge to start taking better care of yourself and here are a few tips for you:

1. **WATCH THE SELF-TALK** - Negative self-talk can increase doubts and fears as well as anxiety so start complimenting yourself more and take time to reflect on your life successes frequently.
2. **BE MORE SELF-COMPASSIONATE** - Be more kind and forgiving to yourself. Allow yourself to make mistakes, move quickly to rebound and learn from them.
3. **BE GRATEFUL** - Being grateful in the now has so much more power than if we focus on the past or chase after the future. Live in the now and be thankful that things are as well as they are.
4. **REWARD YOURSELF** - Let's not forget while praising and gifting others to keep a little for yourself. Reward yourself for big successes and little ones too. However, use discretion in choosing your rewards so as not to create stress in the process.
5. **EXERCISE** - It has amazing power over our body and mind, it can boost your mood, relieve stress and increase confidence. Start small and work up to comfortable and regular periods to insure good health both mentally and physically. Meditation helps too.
6. **EAT WELL** - Balanced meals timed well will insure that you get the nourishment needed to maintain a healthy body and mental attitude. Drink lots of water for a cleaner system.

7. **GET RID OF TOXIC PEOPLE** - Get rid of the people who cause you angst, they are the haters, those who bring negativity into your space. Some you will have to set boundaries for, and others simply delete them. You'll be better for it and so will they.

Reaching a Plateau of Comfortability

The stages of life will go up or down but sometimes it seems to stop in its' tracks. It seems that for whatever reason even though we're still going through the process it ceases to cooperate.

I am in the last stages of a health & wellness program and it seems that I've reached a plateau just when I could begin to really see the results of all my hard work. And as if that wasn't bad enough, I fractured my foot. This now makes exercise near impossible. For a moment, I was reminded of how easy it is to succumb to the tricks of the enemy. Some call him/her satan, our subconscious, the devil, etc. It doesn't really matter the name. What matters is that we realize that something has shifted and then work expeditiously to make it right again.

My plateau this time, was in reaching my fitness goal. What is yours? Are you in a dead-end job, are you sitting on a gift/talent that can benefit others out of fear or because you don't feel worthy? Have you become complacent in being the best mother, father or friend that you can be? Have you become so comfortable in your life with material wealth that you fail to realize the benefits of human wealth which is interacting with new and different people outside your usual circle of family and friends? Growth comes with expanding our territory, reaching beyond our comfort zone. I'm learning new ways to achieve my fitness goals. My foot is only one part of my body so now I just work very gingerly around it. Victory will be mine!

How about you? Are there detours that you need to make to get back on track? You may need to start a whole new route, if so, don't delay for your joy depends on it. Let's leave our regrets in the past and bring a fresh perspective into today, our future. We can do all things through Christ, who, gives us strength. If anyone tells you differently, call them what they are - a liar and certainly not a friend.

It Is All Vanity......

While sitting on the 15th floor patio of a condo and getting some much-needed rest I watched the waves in the gulf as they came in ferociously and receded very calmly; the action was constant. I began to ponder the pattern and then I thought about human beings, we too, are like the gulf - we ebb and flow in this journey called life. We are constantly chasing something, no sooner do we grasp it that it either disappears or becomes meaningless and off we go again. Some grow tired of the chase and check out mentally while others were never equipped for the chase in the first place, so they use any and all means available and necessary only to discover that the mark keeps moving.

What does it really mean? The Scripture says, "The wise man's eyes are in his head; but the fool walketh in darkness: and I myself perceived also that one event happens to them all." (Ecclesiastes-2-14 KJV)

God predetermines the events of life. "To everything there is a season, and a time to every purpose under the heaven. And more over I saw under the sun the place of judgement, the wickedness was there; and the place of righteousness, that iniquity was there. I said in mine heart, God shall judge the righteous and the wicked; for there is a time then for every purpose and for every work." (Ecclesiates 3:1,16-17 KIV)

Until we learn to live in the *now* and let go of our need to control, there can be no peace. Only vanity and it's all vanity.

Chapter 3

Forgiveness

Did You Know? Unresolved Anger is Killing Us

- Unresolved Anger destroys our mind, body and soul when we allow it to fester.
- Unresolved Anger is often confused with unforgiveness and when not treated will rob us of our peace.
- Unresolved Anger brings on stress which damages our health, causing cancer, hypertension, allergies, digestive problems, heart damage and more.
- Unresolved Anger destroys vital relationships, it causes us to bring into new relationships the baggage from previous ones which is the catalyst for yet another dysfunctional family, failed marriage, friendship, partnership, etc.
- Unresolved Anger can destroy relationships among parents and children; it can be so ingrained into the family structure that it is accepted as normal behavior.
- Unresolved Anger leads to destructive behavior - our jails, prisons and mental institutions are filled with persons whose root issue is unresolved anger that is manifesting itself in such ways that cause harm to others. It also causes suicides, self- mutilation, and excess

- /illegal drug use.
- Unresolved Anger will cause our thinking to become so distorted that we begin to see and treat friends, family and other loved ones as enemies.
- Unresolved Anger makes us vulnerable to the world, we'd rather believe a lie than the truth.
- Unresolved Anger, when left untreated kills our own spirit, it makes for a dark and lonely existence.

The challenge is to look deeply within, identify any and all past hurts, accept them as past, let them go and begin to live again.

Anger Creates Holes in Our Heart

Forgiveness is the Free Will to Heal our Heart

Forgiveness is the willingness to let go of and release the hurtful past. It is the decision to no longer suffer, to heal your heart and soul. It is the choice to no longer find value in hatred or anger. And it is letting go of the desire to hurt others, and ourselves, because of something that is already in the past. Forgiveness is not condoning egregious acts nor is it supporting someone else's insane or unjust behavior. Rather, it is an internal process where we execute our free will to heal our own heart and mind.

To forgive is to feel the compassion, gentleness, tenderness, and caring that is always within our hearts, no matter how the world may seem in the moment. Forgiveness is the way to a place of inner peace and happiness, the way to our soul. That place of peace is always available to us, always ready to welcome us in. if, for the moment, we don't see the welcome sign, it is because it is hidden by our own attachment to anger.

Somehow, there is a part of us that believes we can get the peace of mind we seek by holding to hatred, or anger, or pain. There's a part which says that we must protect ourselves and that we can achieve happiness and peace of mind by being attached to hatred and seeking revenge. There's a part of us that says we must withdraw and withhold our love and our joy because we have been hurt in the past.

We can look upon forgiveness as a journey across an imaginary bridge from a world where we are always recycling our anger to a place of peace. That journey takes us into our own spiritual essence and the heart of God. It takes us into a new world of expanding, unconditional love.

Through forgiveness, we receive all that our hearts could ever want. We are released from our fear, anger, and pain to experience oneness with each other and our spiritual Source. Forgiveness is the way out of darkness and into the light. It is our function here on earth, allowing us to recognize ourselves as the light of the world. It allows us to escape the shadow of the past, whether that shadow is our own or another person's. Forgiveness can free us from the imprisonment of fear and anger that we have imposed on our minds. It releases us from our need and hope to change the past. When we forgive, our wounds of past grievances are cleansed and healed. Suddenly we experience the reality of God's love. In that reality, there is only love, nothing else. In that reality, there is never anything to forgive.

Jerry Jampolsky, M.D., Author

When we let go of the anger by choosing to
forgive, we reward ourselves with peace.

A man of great wrath will suffer punishment; for if you rescue him, you will have to do it again. (Proverbs 19:19 KJV)

Don't Let the Deeds of Others Cause You to Lose Your Place in Eternity

Do you become angry when someone breaks a law or offends you or someone you know and love? Do you say things like "I wish they would drop off the face of the earth?" Or "I hate him or her, they should die for what they have done."? If we are breathing and have crossed into the age of adulthood, we have most certainly done something that someone has said or felt one or both of those same things about us.

It is written that we should "judge not, lest we be judged." I wish I knew what was in the mind of those who blatantly perpetrate bad deeds such as a robbery, assault, murder, animal abuse, adultery, hatred, pedophilia, slavery, etc. I wish I knew why **we** do many of the things that we do, even unto ourselves, such as overeating, becoming an alcoholic, an abuser of illegal substances and/or prescribed medications; working too much.... Could it be because we are human; we have unresolved issues as a result of past interactions with others; self-hatred; insecurity; a false sense of protecting oneself?

There are many reasons why this could be and its ok to be angry about the act, to hate it to the core, but, unless we have walked in the shoes of the perpetrator, we cannot know the why of their action. We can judge the act, we can separate ourselves from the person but, we must love them still unless we, ourselves become guilty of sin.

As a mother there are many things that I have witnessed my own children and other family members doing that was inappropriate, but I never stopped loving them. I might have put some distance between us mentally and sometimes even physically, I even made attempts to correct them but inevitably I would choose to pray for them and the situation, freeing myself to continue to love them even the more.

When they continued asking him, he lifted himself, and said unto them, He that is without sin among you, let him first cast a stone at her. (John 1:8 KJV); If we say that we have no sin, we deceive ourselves and the truth is not in us. (1John1:8 KJV) But he who hates his brother is in darkness and walks in darkness, and does not know where he is going, because the darkness has blinded his eyes. (1John 2:11KJV). I love you because you are my brother (sister), not because of your race, political belief, measure of intelligence or attractiveness; you could be in the white house, church house, jail or the street corner it matters not the physical location. What matters is the heart, it's time to take inventory.

We Can't Go Back

Have you ever gone to a restaurant and ordered a specialty dish that you longed to try and when it comes it's everything that you imagined it would be? The presentation is spectacular; the aroma is breathtaking and then you bite into it and WOW! It awakens senses you didn't know you had. And then when the meal is over you walk away feeling as though you've just experienced heaven and you can't wait to come back for that same experience. However, the next experience is not the same….

That's how life is, some of us work our whole lives for a specific event – education, marriage, children, a certain car, our dream home, retirement, wealth, only to find that it's all temporal. We learn and then we forget, marriages end; children become adults; there's a new and better car or home each year. The date for retirement seems to move farther away and wealth is fleeting at best.

Most of these things and events are seasonal. They may be here today and gone tomorrow. Our challenge it seems, is recognizing that when things go, we must move on. That the season has passed and if we maintain the right perspective, we can welcome the new season with enthusiasm and grace.

However, if we insist on looking back, trying to recapture, reinvent and re-imagine yesterday we then create for ourselves negative emotions such as hate, anger, bitterness, discontent, sickness…. We cause loved ones to distance themselves, colleagues and friends to simply tolerate us until they can no longer stand to be around us.

It's very difficult to walk away from something that in our mind and heart has meant so much. But, when seasons change and yes, we know the exact moment and circumstances; we must gird ourselves and let it go. The catalyst that triggers the change could be many things: adultery, fornication, pornography, homosexuality, illicit sex, drugs, alcoholism, over-eating, clubbing overspending, thievery, lying, abuse, wickedness, malice, blasphemy; all these things serve to destroy marriages, children, relationships and our material assets.

People, places and things cannot provide for us what we need the most. What brought satisfaction and delight once may never happen again. It's usually the novelty of a thing -that great meal experience cannot be repeated.

God, the Father is eternal. He is the ultimate relationship. He enables us to see that what we thought was good to us, is bad for us; that our wealth comes in knowing who we are; knowing our value and knowing that in Him, we have everything that we need. Neither sex, food nor money can fill that void.

We must recognize that when the season ends another comes and with it comes some good and some bad and that we need all our energies for that season so we must choose to let go of any and all unfinished business – both good and bad, of the past and walk boldly into the newness of life.

His Resurrection Our Forgiveness

Easter Sunday is the day that many of us commemorate the death and risen Christ. We call it "Resurrection Sunday".

Have you ever wondered where we might be had Christ not withstood the pain and the agony leading up to that day? It is because of Him that we can be free in and of ourselves.

We do ourselves a disservice when we fail to forgive ourselves and others of far less than what Christ endured.

Easter Sunday can be symbolically a day of renewal and refreshing as we choose to release one another from the prisons of unforgiveness and return to love as was commanded by God.

Chapter 4

Restoration – The Cost To Be Free

What Does it Mean to be Free, Really?

Most often when we hear the word "free or freedom" we think of someone being set free from a physical bondage. The reality, however, is that one does not have to be physically bound to lack freedom. Freedom is a state of mind. It matters not where you are nor the conditions if you allow yourself to be imprisoned by your own thoughts, then you are being held captive at will. I have lived long enough and have experienced many challenges to my physical freedom but because I believe that the only person or thing that can break my mental spirit is me, I am still standing today and stronger than ever.

Some of us *celebrate* the 4th of July which is defined in the U.S. as Independence Day, in Rwanda it's Liberation Day, in Zambia it's Unity Day, in the U.S. Virgin Islands it's Emancipation Day.

The common meaning for all of these is "Freedom" but when you look around the world today it seems that much fighting is going on still to achieve true freedom. Why do you think that is? Could it be that we are so focused on achieving the wrong prize? That in our minds this "Freedom" is but an illusion?

Freedom is a state of mind; it has nothing to do with material wealth or physical acquisitions. Freedom is having a love of self and others. It's being ok with who you are and what you have and being happy for others who experience the same and it shouldn't matter that what they may have is different from mine. It is said that the grass seems greener in your neighbor's yard but, you can't see what's required to maintain it. Therefore, we should make ourselves happy with the fruits of our own labor.

The universe brings you what you need and knowing and receiving that within your spirit is true freedom.

Manipulation of the Mind

If you could start today as if there was no past to reference would you choose to be the same? How do you see yourself? Would it be as someone with little or no value? If you could choose between an ancestry of kings and queens -vs- one of slaves would you feel more comfortable in a position of leadership? Would your priorities change from being self-serving to subservient - one who cares for oneself, family and community?

We as a human race, have suffered from mind manipulation for hundreds of years, We have allowed others to define who we are and what we can and cannot be or have. We're doing a disservice to our children by sitting back and enjoying the morsels that are being thrown our way while others are being eaten alive by the same manipulation. One should not be content to simply survive. We are more than conquerors. If we can take little and create much, we can take more and rule the world.

This is not one of those radical speeches to make you want to go out and hurt somebody. This is a reminder that you are powerful sisters and brothers of the human-race. Yes, you owe it to yourself and the future generations who are our children, grand and great-grandchildren to get your act together.

Stop being influenced by the fads of the hour; we have two things that makes us equal in this world. Both are needed by every human being to make them a viable resource - blood and money. The blood gives us life, life gives us a chance. Money gives us options it matters not how much or little we have. What matters is how we use it.

We are bombarded with garbage on a daily basis and are enticed by various mediums to spend our money on things that are temporal such as the many cosmetic (hair accouterments, eye treatments, teeth apparatus, skin and body alterations), earrings in unnatural places; tobacco products and illegal substances as well as over use of prescribed drugs, excess use of alcohol, fancy cars & trucks, expensive radio systems, cheap, and outrageous clothing for example. Others invest their money in stocks, bonds, real estate, family vacations, educational plans for themselves and their children, and they re-invest in their communities by donating money, time and service to worthy organizations and politically.

Don't take my word for this. Commit yourself to one month of observation. Keep a tally of where your money is being spent and with whom it's being spent. Monitor the time (quantity and quality) that you're spending with your children and/or other family members. Define healthy and cost-effective activities, attend classes on finances, banking and investing.

It's time to take charge of the life/lives you've been given charge over. You are more than a conqueror. No man, drug or jail can hold you back. It's all in your hands.

Are You Willing to Be Guided?

For many of us the answer to that question is "not in this lifetime" because we don't think anyone living or dead can know what's best for us. We've been everywhere and tried everything possible to find happiness, to find our place - that thing that makes us complete to no avail. We're willing to blame everyone else for our unhappiness, our mistakes, bad decisions. We spend thousands of dollars on clothing, jewelry, cosmetic surgery, diets, food, doctors and drugs trying to be someone we were never meant to be.

We rob and kill our own parents, children or spouse for reasons that seem so senseless after the fact.

We are not limited to any one race, color or nationality. ***We*** are human beings who bleed the same blood and breathe the same air. What will it take for us to realize that everything that we ***need*** we already have within us, yes, it's nice to have money but, we can only spend so much, and the same is with food, clothing, and other resources.

What we're missing is the most primal of relationships - its "self"- our spirit. Somehow, we lost it in our pursuit of affluence and power; greed in many forms is destroying our very being. Are you tired yet? Are you willing to try something different? Are you willing to give up the fear (loneliness, unforgiveness, guilt, lying, stealing, etc.) to attain wholeness, a newness of life?

Our Creator promises to always guide us; to satisfy our needs; in a land that is baked by the sun He will make us stronger. We will be like a garden that has plenty of water. We will be like a spring whose water never runs dry. All disasters (natural and unnatural) that we're experiencing are not by accident, we are being given notice and the question is How Long? Or What's next? The blessing in being in relationship is that we don't have to worry about the answer to those questions for when our internal being is at peace our external being will not allow fear to take control; to guide our thoughts, feelings and actions. When enough of us are walking in oneness our world will know peace. "I will always show you where to go. I'll give you a full life in the emptiest of places— firm muscles, strong bones. You'll be like a well-watered garden, a gurgling spring that never runs dry." (Isaiah 58:11 Msg)

Small Compromises Can Lead to Devastating Consequences

We all know the quote, "when you know better you do better." But the reality is that we don't always follow that advice. We are often tempted to stray off the mark on our jobs, in our marriages and other relationships, with our children, even our parents for various reasons, all of which at the time seems right; and by the time we realize that a mistake has been made so much has transpired that could have been avoided. If we're lucky we quickly recognize our mistake or mis-judgement and make the necessary corrections or on the other hand we will compromise saying that things are not so bad or 'it could be worse' or that no one is being affected by this but me, Know that there is always someone else other than you who will reap the good or bad of your deeds for, we all are connected to each other.

So, what can we do when our small compromises, mis-judgements begin to destroy our integrity and before it becomes a devastating defeat? We can recognize the situations for what they are and take steps to bring them to an end.

This process for some may be easier said than done and that's when we call in an Advocate, One, (God) who can and will "make a way of escape" for us and will do it without judgement. Having just celebrated the Resurrection of Christ, the gift of atonement is fresh on my mind - that we can acknowledge our faults, confess and be forgiven is the ultimate gift.

Just Look the Other Way

This year has taken off like a rocket, this is that time of year that we're re-organizing our homes, businesses and schedules; we prepare our reports for "Uncle Sam" hoping that we'll get a good return or at least break even.

This is also a good time to reorganize or at least inspect our heart (soul), ask the questions "what things could we have done differently?" "How could we have responded differently to a request, act or deed that may have saved the life or esteem of another person?" I ask myself those questions on a regular basis. I've missed so many opportunities to help others to make a "life" decision because I didn't want to lose their friendship, hurt their feelings, or get involved. It was much easier to just look the other way and wait for someone else to address the issue or hope that it or they would just go away. Galatians 6:1 NIV says "Doing Good to all 6 brothers and sisters, if someone is caught in a sin, you who live by the Spirit should restore that person gently. But watch yourselves, or you also may be tempted."

Now we know that everyone is not going to accept an opportunity of restoration, but we are obligated by the Word to offer it. I can assure you that most often than not the majority will, and the others will certainly think about it when they choose to make a "death" decision. A "Life" decision brings peace, joy and love and radiates from one person to another while a "death" decision brings loneliness, fear and distrust; which gift would you rather give or receive for that matter?

I choose *Life* and having made that choice I will work diligently to bring "life" to as many people from every age, race and economic genre as I can. I invite you to make a choice today, one of restoration for self and others. Don't look away, look to God for His forgiveness and grace.

The Bridge Goes Both Ways

The question is often asked, "Why do you waste your time with people who do bad things?" Jesus said, "he who is without sin cast the first stone", He also said "therefore if your enemy hungers, feed him; If he thirsts, give him a drink; For in so doing you heap coals of fire on his head. Do not be overcome by evil but overcome evil with good."

My answer is that you simply can't live in a community and expect change to come without exerting some energy to make it happen, there are a lot of good people who have been thrown away because of the foolish decisions they've made, if we throw everyone away, we may find ourselves in that pile someday.

Therefore, it behooves us all to reach out and bring as many as we can back into the fold. In serving, we have learned so much about real love, sacrifice and pain. We count our blessings daily and look forward to the next opportunity.

Quote

"Give a man a fish and he will eat for a day, teach him to fish and he will eat for a lifetime."
Chinese Proverb

Love is in the Air

Valentine's Day is but a by-product and seasonal event that some of us look forward to every year. In these times of uncertainty when devastation is happening all around us, we are led to reach beyond our own circle of familiarity to those in foreign lands both near and far. How can we do that without giving it a second thought?

We are a compassionate people; we realize that we are not immune to being next in line for a same or worse event happening in our own back yard. We learn more and more everyday about our connection to one another, even if it's only a spiritual connection. I'm reminded of the outpouring of support that we have been blessed to receive. The feedback that we receive from those whom we serve has demonstrated that we are indeed making a difference in the jails and in our communities; the love you give whether it's through financial or physical contributions helps to restore faith in humanity, in the young and old alike.

We recently hosted a Career Fair for a group of high school students, the spike in their self- esteem levels were evident by the days' end all because of those special people who took a special interest in them for a few hours, some of them were still talking about it when I saw them days later on various occasions. We don't always know how much a smile, hug or kind word (verbal or written) can change attitudes and circumstances for another person. Love knows and when we allow it to have its way, lives are changed, hearts are mended and so the world becomes a better place.

It's A New Season

It seems that just as we get the flowers that we've planted to begin producing their beautiful blooms and the grass to turn that perfect shade of green, the seasons change. The blooms fall away, and the grass becomes a dull green before turning brown.

Such is life. We experience seasons in our lives also. It seems that all is going well for us and then, something tragic will happen, an accident or burglary or death, divorce, loss of employment, illness or a child will lose his/her way. This is not the time to panic or to lose hope. Though the situation may seem too hard to bear at that moment, rest assured that it is only a season. It happened, it hurt, but Joy will come with a New Season. Though the flowers and the green grass only lasted a brief time we were able to enjoy them for that time.

The Seasons in our lives may last a day or several years, however long it may be, we must make the most of them. Everything on this earth is temporal; here today and gone tomorrow. Life is given and life is taken away. What matters is what we do with what we have during that season. If we truly love and cherish the people in our lives and we believe that "all things work together for the good of those who are called according to the purpose of the Father", then, we gracefully let go when its time and await the New Season with great expectation. The memories of the past will be forever embedded in or hearts and our hearts will grow to receive the Present of today. We will still be able to reflect on seasons past; to remember the sweet aroma of the roses; the taste of fresh vegetables from our gardens; the laughter of a loved one.

Seasons are necessary for physical and spiritual growth. Some seasons will be fast and easy while others will seem to last way too long as we experience the challenges which build character and strength.

I am looking forward to what this New Season will have in store for me, not because of who I am, but because of Whose I am. I encourage you to embrace the life that you now live for it is all that you have.

Let go of pride, anger, bitterness, unforgiveness and past regrets; if it was meant to be it would have happened. Freely embrace the newness of life and all that it has to offer. Receive it in the spirit of Love.

*Many girls experience unpleasant relationships with their mother, and as a result,
may experience low self-esteem or anger issues.
I had a lot of anger and unforgiveness toward my
mother because I felt that she failed
to protect me and my sisters.
While searching for answers through prayer the following poem came to me"*

A Letter from Our Mother (in spirit)

Dear Daughter,

I love you with all my heart.
I missed so many opportunities to tell you so
I should have never let us drift apart.

My life has not been easy, mistakes were many.
and though I did the best I could it was not
enough to do you much good

I am your mother; you will only have one.
There may be others who step into the role
and to them, I say "thank you" for all you have done.

Living or dead, the memories are real.
The loss is painful and present still.
Please don't hate me any longer, forgive me if you can.
See me in my broken-ness and for
yourself create a better plan.

MAE DIXON

I love you with all my heart.
You are my daughter, you are much like me, you see.
You are strong, wise, beautiful, compassionate and smart.
Hopefully you will be the mother that I could not be.
Mae Dixon

The Light of My Father

Life has a way of keeping us bound
to a past that we simply can't shake.

Often, I try to figure the ways and whys of it all
and then it's as if there's this dark, dark voice speaking very harshly
saying, "don't go there it will hurt too much."

And then, I hear another voice speaking ever so softly,
in almost a whisper saying, "you must go, do not be afraid
for freedom lies on the other side."

I ask myself, why is it so hard? What have I to lose?
What is there to gain? After much thought, the answer comes.

Much has been lost, love, trust, the need to be held by him -
my father, that is, to hear him say the words "I love you,
I'm here for you, I'm proud of you.

Many a relationship has failed because of the insecurities I feel
within my own self. Yet, that soft voice keeps speaking ever so gently,
reminding me that I, alone am enough.
The darkness has gone away, and the light has come to stay.
The light causes love to illuminate within my heart,

it is healing every hurt, it is healing every disappointment,
it is bringing Joy, Peace, Esteem and Gratitude.

It is here to stay, the light that is. The light of my Father.

Mae Dixon

Chapter 5

Peace

Spirituality

When Was the Last Time....?

We live in a world that is so fast paced that there have been times I couldn't remember if I had slept the night before. Yes, I went to bed probably around 3 a.m. only to rise again at 6 a.m. The mind was racing with multiple tasks and situations with which to contend, but my body would respond "Really?" I'm ashamed to say that this went on for far too long.

One morning during my quiet time I heard a voice whisper the question, "when was the last time you simply sat in your favorite chair and read a book just for the fun of it, not because you needed to prepare for a program or work or a school assignment, but just because you wanted to? When was the last time you went for a stroll or jog in your favorite park or the one in your neighborhood on a sunny day and experience the rustling of the trees as the squirrels and birds raced from one tree to the other as they play without a care in the world; or stop by the nearest waterfront (the bay, beach, lake, etc.) during a rain and watch the dynamics played out in the sky and upon the water?

I pondered this question and had to confess it's been a while since I did anything that didn't have a deadline. Those are simple inexpensive joys that I've missed and to have it brought to my attention I realized that my body was missing it also. I realized that the mind while very logical most of the time lacks emotion; therefore, we need to program into it a plan for rest and relaxation, not the kind that comes when there's been a few drinks, too much food or pure exhaustion occurs. The mind got to going again this time I thought about what happens when we have or take too much time to rest. Are we missing out on opportunities of a different kind of joy? The joy of being of service to others; to be useful? Too much time spent in solitude with self gives way to negative thoughts and feelings of helplessness, loneliness, unworthiness, illness and or depression.

There are times that we use busyness to compensate for or ignore more serious issues. We use it as a shield or excuse to avoid confrontations and situations that we perceive to be overwhelming only to realize that what we've "perceived" in our mind is much greater than what is. Where do we begin with addressing our lifestyle of today? Do we stop and take control of the situation or do we wait for sickness to dictate our future, maybe we should stop today, take pen in hand and list the ways we spend our time; place a value on each activity; the value can be monetary or emotional. If you find that less than 20% of your day is spent in personal time and less than 25% is spent in sleep, then you're out of balance.

I made a personal decision that this new year would be different. The results of my assessment were very unbalanced so I took the steps listed to determine how best to regain or implement the actions needed to attain a balance that would provide me with a healthy, joyful and effective lifestyle; a lifestyle that would positively impact my life and the lives of others. Now, how about you? When was the last time that you did something good and special for yourself or someone else just because?

Favor is Not Fair

Recently, while having breakfast at a restaurant, a young mother and her two children were seated next to me. The mother took the children (a boy, approx. 6 and girl, approx. 4 yrs. old) to get their food and brought them back to the table and very patiently served them, offering them their choice of seats, cutting up their food and inquiring about any additional needs. Confident that they were settled she told them she would be right back and walked away.

The two of them chatted back and forth for a while as though this was a normal occurrence; after a while the little girl became concerned because mom had been gone for a while now. She started to look around anxiously and finally leaned over to her brother and asked, "where is mama?" At this point I tried to ease her anxiety by explaining that mom had gone to get her breakfast and would return shortly.

About this time mom appeared with an omelet and the little girl with misty eyes asked, "Mommy, what took you so long?" She didn't even wait for an answer she resumed to chatter away with her brother.

When the mother finished eating, she made sure that the children were satisfied and proceeded to help first, the boy down from the table; the girl looked at her with folded arms and asked, "why didn't you get me down first?" The mom replied, "because I got your brother down first" and proceeded to help the girl down from her chair. The girl looked at her, arms still folded across her chest with a very sour tone and tears running down her face and said," that's not fair, I should have been first." 'The mother replied, "what difference does it make, I helped you down too didn't I?"

This seems to be the attitude of many adults today, we think that because of our position or status, our looks, our place in the family, that we should be automatically entitled to certain things (promotions, inheritances, gifts, etc.) but this is not so in the spirit realm, there is no special formula because Favor is not Fair. God rains on the just as well as the unjust and because we as humans are not privileged to know His conditions or reasons for showing favor to someone that we may deem unworthy does not prevent Him from doing so.

Resolve to Evolve

Some days I awake and ask "Lord, what's next?" and then there are other days that I ask "Father, do we have to do this now, today?"

What I learned long ago is that it's not *my will* that count, but His. His will wields a power unlike anything that I could ever imagine. His will turns my "I can't" into an "I can".

Why is it so difficult for us to resolve to evolve? Is it because of fear that our evolution will result into something negative or that it could possibly be the reverse, positive?

To remain in our comfort zone is an effortless achievement, but to evolve into an unknown state would require that we think and act differently; it would require that we forget past hurts, losses and even some achievements; to do so would mean that we can no longer blame others for our behavior or lack of success. We would have to love unconditionally, reject negative thoughts, restrain from behaving negatively and forgive.

To evolve would require our reaching in to reach out. How about it, can you resolve to evolve? Do you wonder if there's more for you on the other side of the curtain of life? Do you experience a feeling of incompleteness, a wanting/yearning for more of the unknown? Evolution is inevitable, we have the power to say yes to it and enjoy the journey. Say Yes Today.

Quote

For I know the plans I have for you," declares
the L̲o̲r̲d, "plans to prosper you
and not to harm you, plans to give you hope and a future.
(Jeremiah 29:11 NIV)

Who Are You Following?

I find that in this day and time this question needs to be asked more so now than ever before. We live in a time where there are so many options, many, though they may seem to be tremendous opportunities, once given a closer look prove to be unhealthy and an adverse testimony to who we say that we are. Who, are your sphere of influence? Do they impact your life in a positive way? Can you honestly say that your life has been enriched as a result of their presence or do you feel as though you've lost something during the interchange?

    I recently experienced a situation that I feel almost cost me my salvation; my integrity was put to the test and for a second, I almost lost it. Someone for whom I had the highest amount of respect and admiration was called on to use their authority to help someone else gain a coveted position and to do so required my cooperation. I liked this other person and really wanted to help them even though I felt that it was not the best move for them. I took some time to pray about the situation, and it was decided that I could not support the effort. I knew that when I conveyed my decision it would cause some hard feelings and it did.

    Its times like these we must count the cost, be it a friendship, family member, marriage or self. Sometimes, we are our own worst enemy, we allow our flesh to dictate our actions and are then confronted with devastating consequences. Be sure that the person in whom you place your ultimate confidence is one who will lead and guide you to a place of perfect peace both mentally and physically. There will always be promises of more money, power or material assets, but the true prize requires clean hands and a pure heart. Now look to those in your circle, and those to whom you seek direction and leadership, do they challenge you to be your best self or do they encourage you to settle for mediocrity? Someone is looking to you for leadership, for direction as they navigate this maze called life, it could be a child or an elder; are you up to the challenge?

Where Are You Resting

The next time someone asks you "how are you doing?" Think it, even if you don't say it, "I'm resting in Jesus as he gets me ready for my next level." Though it may sound churchy or corny, think about it. We have a choice to be well or to be sick; to be joyful or sad; thankful or selfish; to love or to hate; to fight or submit.

A peaceful spirit is happy in Jesus, a contrite spirit is not happy and will not rest until everyone around them joins them in their misery. Which one are you?

To rest in Him (Jesus), is to cast all your cares (financial woes, health problems, marital or singleness challenges) on Him. It means to give it to our Father, and Let It Go; Faith means to believe that He's got it and knows better than we how to handle it.

To Rest in Him is to go about with a smile in our heart, a dance in our step, a kind word or deed for a stranger....

This doesn't mean that I'll have money all the time, that my body will never hurt again; that everyone will love me or do right by me. What it does mean is that for as long as I'm resting in Him, it won't matter, for peace reigns, in the midst, of a storm.

Chapter 6

Hope: To be Restored by Grace and Love: A Thirst that Water Can't Fill

A Little Help Goes A Long Way

Upon arrival at the Restoration Center, a middle-aged gentleman was sitting in front of my office. I asked if I could help him; he had the most peaceful aura about him. His clothing was in disarray but, he was very confident, joyful, it seemed. He remarked, "Oh, I'm just waiting for the center to open; I'm having a bit of a challenge and need a little help. You see, I recently got laid off my job of 16 years, lost my retirement in the stock market, lost my home and health insurance.

He further stated, "I'm trying desperately not to lose my hope, for it's all that I have left. I'm not looking for a handout, just a little help to take me a little further until I can see my way clear."

I assured him that we could do something to help him.

As I continued into my office, I was thinking to myself that none of us are above being in this man's shoes. I reflected on the families in Alabama and Mississippi who in one moment were enjoying their homes and in only seconds later had it all taken away by a tornado. Many even lost their lives.

These are just a few reminders of how much we take for granted; how quickly we forget from whence we have come. Day in and day out we encounter women and men who have been devastated by the challenges of life, sometimes just the gift of a bus ticket to get to a doctor's appointment, job interview or to the food stamp office is like gold in the hand of a prospector.

Let's Continue to Build the Road

So many stepped up after my plea to help support our work.

We are grateful for the generosity and the quick response. Isaiah 62:10 KJV says "Go through, go through the gates; prepare ye the way of the people; cast up, cast up the highway; gather out the stones; lift up a standard for the people."

We cannot give up on those who are yet struggling to find their way. To love is not expressed in what we say but rather it's in what we do. To see a mother rummaging through a garbage bin in search of food for her children, who are playing (oblivious to their true plight) a few yards away. To the father, who, because of numerous bad decisions has no home in which to return so he wanders from city to city, shelter to shelter.

To the murderer, the pedophile, the thief, the abuser, the alcoholic, the drug addict, the overeater, the repressed and depressed, the question is constant, "Where is the light? How much longer can I go on? Where is this God that I hear so much about but can't see? Does anyone care that I'm hurting? That my sin is a result of my pain?"

We are the light, those of us who ungrudgingly give of our time, our resources, our finances and our prayers. We are the messengers of Peace, of Hope and of Charity. We acknowledge that we, too have fallen short of perfection; we've made mistakes that have caused harm to others and because of a gracious Father we were given another chance. That is good news! Do continue to give with an open heart. We can't allow fear to paralyze us or to create hate for one another. Our Father teaches that we should hate the sin but love the sinner as we do ourselves.

The scripture referenced above is taken from the Free on the Inside Bible, a translation for those who are held prisoner to a life without hope, that could be anyone of us should we fail to stay connected to the Source.

If you are not a part of this Road Building project, I encourage you to sign up today to help remove the stones and raise the banner alerting the masses of our coming King.

Count it All Joy

When it seems that all is lost that is when we call upon our reserve, buckle up and settle in for the ride. If we listen to the news and not rely on the report of the Lord, we will surely fail. When it seems that the world is about to self- destruct that is the time for the believers to gather together and strengthen each other. It is also the time to reach out to those who are struggling in their faith or who are trying to find their way. I am in awe of the ways in which we are constantly being protected from the wiles of the devil.

There is so much going on around us. Families are being tested with illness, the unexpected and tragic death of loved ones, financial woes due to layoffs and foreclosures, and yet we're still standing. We are more than conquerors, we know that ***things*** can be replaced, that this earthly life is cyclical, that seasons past and with spring comes new life.

You Can Change Your Mind

It is time to change the way we think and not allow others to dictate our thoughts. Nothing lasts forever and though our circumstances may seem hopeless or we feel that where we are now is where we'll always be or worse. I challenge you to change your mind and re-focus your thoughts on a new and better life.

We feel blessed to be able to share with you each month, but we're hopeful that someday you will come in to *bring* something to share with others who are where you are today. Now, if that never happens, it's ok with us. We will serve you joyfully for as long as our resources are available.

As a young girl I would see my mother coming home broken and tired each day with a bag just like the ones we give to you. I had no idea where the food came from or what it had cost her to get it. As I got older and began to understand better, I vowed that life for me would be different. I made some mis-steps starting out, but in my determination to have a different story as I grew older, I sought out people, places and things that would help me to get in a position to not only help others, but teach others to help themselves.

In order to do that I had to envision what that looks like. To accomplish it I had to first let go of my prideful attitude and receive the help that challenged me to use my mind rather than simply accept meager handouts which usually consisted of "just enough" to satisfy my immediate needs, but never enough for the long term.

It doesn't matter who you are, your age, your race, nationality or religion, what matters is that you recognize that you are better than your circumstances; that where there's a will to achieve a better life a way is already made. You simply need to want it bad enough to go after it. We have a little because we don't demand more; we don't demand more because we don't feel worthy. We're told that the future is bleak, things are only going to get worse, and for some, it may, but you don't have to be in that number.

May you experience an abundance of peace and joy as you seek a more excellent way.

Reconnecting – What Was Old is New Again

These past few weeks I've reconnected with a lot of old friends, both personally and professionally. We've spent hours catching up on the accomplishments, personal challenges, our children's achievements and our future hopes and dreams. I thought about how easy it was to pick up where we'd left off some 3,5 even 10 years ago. Lunch gatherings turned into an afternoon visit while phone calls lasted for 1-2 hours; the parting came with still so much left to talk about that promises were made to get together again much sooner than later.

Our Heavenly Father reminds us in His Word of the importance to assemble ourselves together to strengthen one another yet, we allow the cares of this world to bring division, to separate us from the very source Who can and will sustain us, protect and provide for us. Thankfully, the way is made that no matter how far away we are, there's a road that leads back to home; to heart; to Love.

I'm reminded of a time as a child, while out with my mom, she encountered an old friend; the friend greeted her with a big smile and hug and said," it's been such a long time, so come on over here and give an account of yourself." She wanted to be brought up to date on my mom's life. Our Heavenly Father is like that old friend, although He's Omniscient and Omnipresent, He wants to spend time with us, He wants to hear from us what's been happening in our lives. He wants us to confess our hurts, our fears; to share our victories, our hopes and dreams. He wants to embrace us and assure us that all will be well no matter how bad it seems in the natural.

These are perilous times that we're living in - wars and rumors of wars; earthquakes and great storms; terrorism is at an all-time high. But fear not for there is a hiding place and that place is in the arms, the shelter of the Almighty God. "God *is* our refuge and strength,

A very present help in trouble. Therefore we will not fear, Even though the earth be removed,

And though the mountains be carried into the midst of the sea; *Though* its waters roar *and* be troubled, *Though* the mountains shake with its swelling. Selah." (Psalm 46:1-3 NKJV)

There is nothing new under the sun, the need for love is constant; the love for God and the love for each other so, as we navigate this course called life let us remember to reconnect often with loved ones and to not be afraid to forge new relationships thereby building bridges that can and will sustain us in our times of need.

Who's Loving You?

The question is, "who's loving you?" February is LOVE month for most, but for some it is anything but. For some it is the most depressing time of the year and especially so if there is no significant love interest in their lives. That is, one that they can touch and see. And on the flip side there are those who are in relationships where constant contact is present, but the love is gone or was never present. So, what can be done to create some joy in the Love month and beyond? ***LOVE YOURSELF!*** We should never allow another person to define for us who we are. However, we must be certain that we know who we are and what it is that we desire, and not just from a romantic partner but, from ourselves, our family and friends. Loving oneself is a holistic process that extends beyond the external. It begins internally both mentally, emotionally and spiritually.

The process of loving yourself is to first be okay with you; to love yourself despite the mistakes of the past, to make peace with the past and this includes the hurt and pain inflicted at the hands of others, be it intentional or otherwise.

We were never designed to live in a bubble, we were made by a loving God. We were made to love and be loved. God's love for us is perfect and unconditional yet, we can generally find all kinds of reasons to deny ourselves. Could it be that we feel undeserving of such a pure love and as such are willing to settle for less than favorable signs of affection which inevitably brings us to this desperate and/or depressed state?

If *you're loving you* today, I challenge you to not be selfish with your love. Share the love with others and not just with those with whom you know, who look and act like you. Reach out and share some love with your neighbor across the street, the store clerk who is having a bad day, the sick, infirmed, and incarcerated, a misbehaving child, a frustrated mother. In return our heavenly Father will shower you with an everlasting love, such that will fill you to overflowing.

Focus on Who You Love

Many of us are in a place where we are simply existing - going through the motions of living but not really living. We are allowing what happens around us to influence who we are and find that we're not experiencing the joy and the richness that true living provides.

Recently I had the opportunity, so I made the commitment to connect with family and friends. I succeeded in most instances and did one better by spending some quality time with a special cousin. It was truly a God-moment.

Life is so fragile and yet we take it for granted by letting it flitter by mindlessly. And then, the day comes when we realize that 20, 30, 50 years have passed and there's barely anything of substance to show for those years.

Who do you love? What are you doing about it? How does the subject of your love know that you're loving them? If it's you, how do you give special attention to your deepest needs or fears? Do you take the time to reflect on what's really happening to you, for you? If it's someone else, how do you show them that they are important to you, that they matter? What of you do you give to them, or is it simply a take/take relationship? Are you so engaged in working, being a caretaker for others that there's no time left for you or others who need you, if only to acknowledge that they exist?

My visit with family and friends helped me to realize what is important to me and for me. It helped me to remember that we are so desperately in need of love, self-love. Not selfish love but soulful love; we must lose the facades, drop the masks and give ourselves permission to feel the love for who we are now and not try to be someone else for others. Teach others to love you for who you are, only then can you truly experience the joy and richness of living a life of meaning. As we mature our capacity for love will change but it never dies. We often must work to keep it fresh but work we must, and this is love as it relates to our significant other, our parents, siblings, extended family and friends also. The value of material things is temporal but our love, not so much. For as long as we have breath in our bodies love is present and it begins with the love of our Creator for us and then spreads abroad. Don't wait until you've lost someone to acknowledge their value to you. Who do you love? Tell them and tell them often.

A Thirst that Water Can't Fill

The summer heat makes us thirsty. It makes us more thirsty than usual and as such we consume larger quantities of various beverages in our efforts to quench our thirst. There's another kind of thirst that causes us to seek fulfillment – it's a spiritual thirst. It goes beyond the physical and becomes very intimate, sometimes to the point of becoming painful because in our effort to satisfy it we tend to try various external remedies and techniques.

Our spirit aids us in our ability to love first, ourselves and then others, and in order to do that we must give it what it needs which is a steady dose of wisdom from the word of God, our creator. We can tell when we're running low because we tend to tire easily in our service to self and others. We make excuses instead of progress in our daily lives; we find it more difficult to tolerate one another and we look externally for a solution when the solution is internal.

Like newborn babies we should crave – thirst for the pure spiritual milk, that by it we may be nurtured and grow into maturity. I Peter 2:2 NIV (paraphrased)

It is the wisdom from the creator that will unlock every door in our life, it will turn every failure into success. Let us go beyond the surface (our mind, heart) into the spirit where the true nourishment will flow from Him (The Holy Spirit) into our spirit. There we will find peace, joy, self- love and selfless love for others.

Chapter 7

Purpose: Do Something

To Live Full, Die Empty

The cemetery is the riches place in the world because people fail to leave their precious resources to others.

If You're alive, you were born
To do something.

Discover your Purpose for living,
Then Do It!

Reflections

To be Called or Chosen - A Light for the Nations

I remember going to school for the first time and being *called* upon to speak on a specific topic; little did I know that at the time what being called really meant. Then there was the time that through no effort of my own, I was the one *chosen* out of the whole class to lead for the entire week! Initially my ego soared, grandiose ideas were flittering around in my head of all the things I would be doing until, the assignment was underway. What was thought to be a prestigious appointment turned out to be anything but.

To be called is to be set apart for service; to relinquish your will to that of a higher calling. In the classroom, it's the teacher; in the earth realm it's God, our Father. There is no place for ego among the called; one must serve with humility and discipline, steadily pouring out of oneself for all others in acts of love. (Ephesians 4:1-6 NIV- As a prisoner for the Lord, then, I urge you to live a life worthy of the calling you have received. [2] Be completely humble and gentle; be patient, bearing with one another in love. [3] Make every effort to keep the unity of the Spirit through the bond of peace. [4] There is one body and one Spirit, just as you were called to one hope when you were called; [5] one Lord, one faith, one baptism; [6] one God and Father of all, who is over all and through all and in all.) The chosen are instruments of God, doing His work and speaking out for Him; telling others (the sick, the lame, the orphan, the poor, the hungry, the homeless) of the night-and-day difference He made for them - for us; from nothing to something, from rejected to accepted. For this is the will of our Father. (1Peter 2:9-10 NKJV paraphrased)

We must continue to work while it is day, not allowing thoughts of the "end times" to paralyze us but, rather see it as an opportunity to right some wrongs; to live a life that is meaningful, on purpose; without shame or prejudice. For many we will be the only light that they will see, and therefore must endeavor to keep it shining even when it seems impossible to do so. Answering the call to serve the misguided, abused, neglected and poor among us was the best decision I have ever made. Yes, I get tired in the work but never tired of the work for I see the hand of God all over it. I see Him using the downtrodden to strengthen me and me (and all who serve with me) to give them hope and a future.

The changing of the season is a good time to contemplate what's in store for our own future, to ask the question "how can I make a difference in the lives of others?" As you seek guidance and discernment. As we prepare for a new year, more transitioning will take place enabling us to maintain and even improve upon the level of service that we provide. We must stay on the wall until the work we were called to do is completed.

Do Something

> "He who observes the wind and waits for
> all conditions to be favorable will not sow,
> and he who regards the clouds will
> not reap." Ecclesiastes 11:4 AMP

We, as a people are expected to do something that will produce good fruit. We sometimes also expect to reap a harvest when or where we have failed to sow. We're living in a time and place where it will take every abled body doing his or her part to help restore our sense of peace in this world and in our communities. We cannot sit back and point the finger at our neighbor, our employer or statesman and say, "you must do something." The time is now for you and me to stand up and speak out and be counted as one who demands that civility, compassion and respect be restored to our country, our homes, communities and schools.

We must personally also be responsible to ourselves first and then to those with whom we share a home and/or love relationship. Some of us have taken our "freedom" for granted, we have created a "no limits" kind of mentality where integrity, faithfulness and accountability has been placed on a shelf and an attitude to "just do me" has risen. Imagine a future filled with people whose only goal is to serve themselves; whose only concern is for "me and mine". What happens then to the rest of the country, the world? Everyone cannot fit into that category, nor should we want to. We are commanded to live in love with and for one another.

Please don't miss your opportunity to speak and be heard, to do and be seen; to sow and then reap a bountiful harvest. After all, it's our soul's purpose for being here.

Make the Most of this Season of Repositioning

Repositioning is the shifting of a person, place or thing; it is to shake up that which has become stagnant; to move to another level. The changing times has forced many of us to reposition ourselves as a result of job loss, sickness, death of a loved one, foreclosure, bankruptcy and the list goes on. For some, Repositioning is a voluntary action, whether it takes place in our personal or professional life, the results will impact our future.

In society today, many people have this mindset that they should always be doing something. Daniel 12:4 KJV states, "But thou, O Daniel, shut up the words, and seal the book, even to the time of the end: many shall run to and fro, and knowledge shall be increased." While it is important to be proactive, just staying busy doesn't guarantee fruitful lives. I see this recent move of our organization as part of my own personal Repositioning, this move has caused others to re-think their positions as well. As for me, the evolution of this work is inevitable, and part of the process is to expand the vision and its reach by incorporating the gifts and talents of a diverse group of believers. I can already see my load becoming lighter enabling me to be more proficient where it matters most.

How does one know when it's time to Reposition? Well, I can only speak for me, but I believe that when we allow ourselves to become one with our Source (for me He is God) we will know when it's time to shift. To do this we must take the time away from everything to just be in His presence and we can't do that if we are busy 24/7. I find that taking just 20 minutes twice daily to sit quietly not only refreshes my spirit, it heals old hurts and provides clarity during times of uncertainty. There is nothing new under the sun, we can be sure that we can and will be victorious if we make informed and prayerful decisions. We should not be afraid to step outside our comfort zone any more than we should hide our head in the sand when things seem unfamiliar or difficult. So, don't allow fear to stunt your growth, no matter how badly things may seem today remember that you have the power to do great and miraculous things.

Are you a Fire Origin Species?

Are you a fire starter or trendsetter? Are you like the pinecone that falls to the ground and is sealed shut until someone comes along and starts a fire that melts away the seal allowing your seeds to finally grow?

I've been called by some, a "fire starter" because I've started many things that others have said can't be done and watched them be taken over by others and they be given the credit for the original idea. A fire starter in most instances will not get to see their idea blossom to its full capacity under his/her own care. Their job is simply to plant the seed/get the fire started.

A fire starter is a visionary, a person who is ahead of his/her time, a person with original ideas about what the future will or could be like; has big ideas, are creative by nature. Crazy ideas, but forward-thinking ideas — ideas that just might change the way the world works. A fire starter/visionary may be looked upon as a threat to those in power if, they aren't confident in their own ability, but a fire starter can also be an asset when given the opportunity to share his/her talents.

Some or most fire starters have experienced adverse (trauma) situations; they may have been born into adversity - maybe physically or emotionally challenged. They are generally more inclined to take a chance on life. On the other hand, one might be the pinecone who waits for someone else to get them started, who lives a fearful existence.

That doesn't mean that they are any less important or necessary to fulfil the plan for our existence.

However, fear has a way of stifling our growth, it prevents or delays our opportunity for realizing our full potential. One can't look at a person and determine their true nature unless of course, you're gifted to do so. Which fire origin species are you? Is there any room for new growth in your future?

My Life Is Not My Own

For as long as I can remember, I would try to conform to what others wanted me to be (with a few exceptions, of course) but, it just didn't feel right [for me]. It seemed that the more I would conform, the more I'd feel like a stranger in a foreign land. I just didn't fit. I've been described by some as different or peculiar, strange, a rebel....

I often wondered why it was that I could not just blend into my surroundings? I didn't feel that I was better than others, only that something was out of sync, even my siblings labeled me "different".

For some time, I attributed it to Low Self Esteem due to my past of mental & physical abuse, poverty and even race at times. The reality was and still is that I made a choice as a child to live for Who I believed then and even more so now to be the Risen Savior. It was because of Him, the Great Physician, that I was able to endure the pain, heartbreak, embarrassment and other distresses both then and now, and still be able to stand.

Yes, I SOLD OUT! I am not my own. I live, move and have my being only because of Him and therefore I owe my all to Him. Afterall, He gave His all for me! I know now that it's ok if I don't "fit" into certain circles, places or in the doing of certain things. What's important is that I (we) love all humankind regardless of race, creed, color, financial status, religious or political belief.

Jesus died the ultimate death so that we might live free from sin, live abundantly and into eternity

Chapter 8

Grace: I Feel Love from You

I'm Thankful Because....

In 2002, my heavenly Father gave me the gift of forgiveness. He showed me that through Him every hurt could be healed, every broken heart could be mended, and every bad memory could be erased, forgotten, gone forever. He showed me that by helping others to see that they too could be free mentally and physically through Him, that I would know a peace that surpasses all understanding.

I'm thankful for a family who loves me as I am. Who are willing to stand with me through thick and thin?

I'm thankful for the respect and the fellowship of friends and professional associates who still greet me with love even though the times that I see them anymore is very infrequent due to the very nature of my calling.

I'm thankful for the men, women and children that we serve daily, they help me to remain humble, to remember to count my blessings when I think about days gone by.

I'm thankful for the people in law enforcement who put their lives on the line in our community daily for our safety.

I'm thankful for our Armed Forces who keep watch over our borders and protect us from the evils of the world.

I'm thankful for those of you who have supported this work financially, physically and prayerfully. Its' been quite a journey, its' been life changing to watch the transformation of so many men and women. Thank You.

The Sufficiency of Grace

The grace of our Father is Sufficient. We waste so much valuable time fretting over things that we have absolutely no control over. We despise our small beginnings and envy the blessings of others and when we finally get that which we felt we couldn't live without and all the baggage that arrives with it, only then can we see that our Father was giving us grace in the situation. We often wonder why and how some people can live in the situations that they do; how can they be content with so little, how can they drive up and down the roadways in their electronic scooter with a smile on their face or push a buggy filled with all their belongings from sun up to sun down?

While I have heard many a testimony from people who were not living "their best life", this past week and a half has shown me a new level of poverty while serving the children during the Summer Food Program. It is heart wrenching to watch mothers come through the door with their children making sure that they get to eat while they, themselves are starving. We literally force some of them to take a specially prepared "parent snack pack" because they are trying to save face in the presence of their children. We use this opportunity to give mom a break each day along with the oldest sibling who feels obligated to fill mom's role in her absence. We find that by doing so it reduces the stress levels of everyone and makes for more peace and less violence in the homes.

The children receive a healthy meal and get to play games and learn some very important life skills in the process. We held our semi-annual

Community Food Give-Away serving more than 120 families and many homeless men and women. We could not have impacted so many without the help of our church family and community partners. This event took place outside of our Center that offers emergency assistance on weekdays, this event was designed to put food on the tables of those mothers who are existing on meager fare and are trying to maintain a home for their babies, senior citizens and persons with disabilities and others who met the USDA requirements. One might ask how "does this fit into your mission of restoring lives and rebuilding families?"

Grace is defined as "the unearned or unmerited kindness, mercy and forgiveness of God." II Corinthians 12:9 NIV states "But he said to me, "My grace is sufficient for you, for my power is made perfect in weakness. "Therefore, I will boast all the more gladly about my weaknesses, so that Christ's power may rest on me."

My grace is sufficient for thee; for my strength is made perfect in weakness." A very simple illustration would be that of a man who is already humiliated because he cannot work to support his family but re-gains some sense of manhood when he is given a renewed measure of hope and can carry home to his family food to eat. Or a mother who have lost all measure of self- esteem because of the degrading things she has done simply to survive and then learn that there is still hope for her when she is shown options for starting over again. Or the children who receives special attention now because their mom who is incarcerated and trying to improve her life is now reaching out to them through newfound friends via the "woman to woman" program. Grace is the love God shares through you and me when His will is done.

Reflections of Gratitude

I was seeking change recently for twenty dollars a gentleman offered me 10 - $2.00 bills, my eyes lit up and I shared with him that I used to collect those. He said, "oh well they are readily available now, I just went to the bank and asked for them and received them." I went to the market after that for some veggies and paid my tab using the $2 bills, the cashier lit up. He asked, "are you a lucky person?" I said no, but I am blessed. He then said, "when I get off tonight, I'm going to buy these $2 bills from my boss and let your luck, uh, blessedness will rub off on me. I smiled and began to think, if only it was that easy. Being *Blessed* is a state of mind, it is not something you can buy. I left that market in tears just thinking about how blessed I really am. Just when I thought my life was about to be over, I was given a fresh start in a new city, with a new church family, renewed health; my heart was opened to new adventures, I authored my first book, I am now using my gifts in two cities/counties......

We typically take for granted the simple things in life and see the significant ones as being a result of luck, but luck only brings temporary and often superficial results. Blessings are much more lasting and meaningful when placed in their proper perspective. I find myself offering up gratitude when I arrive at an intersection and I can cross without interference from on-coming traffic or when I hear the laughter of a child innocent of the danger that lurks nearby or when a stranger looks at me and smile or make casual conversation; I offer up gratitude when I awake in the morning and realize that I still have breath, can see, hear, smell and taste, and when I sit at the end of the day and watch the sunset.

Thanksgiving, the holiday is a time of reflection, time to be with family and create traditions. Every day that we live we should find at least one thing to be thankful for and then go a step further by sharing with others out of our abundance. That abundance is not limited to money, it can be time or service.

Chapter 9

Mission Fulfilled

There was a time in my life when I felt that the whole world was caving in on me. Try as I might to do all the right things my reward seemed to be more pain, turmoil and angst. Then after becoming so full of self-pity that I could no longer stand myself I began to pray. Not that I hadn't been praying all along, but this time was different. This time it was a prayer of total surrender, a prayer of humility, of submission to simply let go and let God.

I wondered later, why had I waited so long; what did I hope to accomplish in my own power, my own will? By surrendering my will to God's will I learned that the possibilities for my life were limitless; that all I had been doing was wallowing in self-pity, waiting on someone else to complete me, to do for me what was for me to do myself. I learned that I could be flying among the clouds. I could be positioning myself for the great future that was promised to me at birth, but instead, I was angry because others were not making it happen for me.

Today I fly freely - in Jesus, and it's all because I've accepted who and whose I am. I've accepted that my only responsibility to others is to love them as my Father loves me and to stay true to myself. My childhood was a very difficult one, one that could have caused me to turn out very differently but, having developed a relationship with God at an early age thanks to my mom, I was able to stand strong when many of my friends tried to take me in a different direction.

When God gave me the assignment to provide a refuge for women who were homeless, imprisoned and hopeless, I thought to myself, "He's got the wrong girl", and even questioned his judgement. I couldn't believe that He would trust me with such a mission. He reminded me of my trauma-filled childhood and early adult years and then my favorite scripture, "I can do all things through Christ, who strengthens me." (Philippians 4:13 KJV)

I then began to do what I do best; write the vision. I shared it with those closest to me, they were a little reluctant to follow me into this one. A few faithful family members and friends knew that I would not stop until I at least tried to fulfill the mission. Many times, I started to retreat to what I do best because this time I was truly treading into foreign territories.

I stayed the course, implemented the women's program in the county jail along with 3 volunteers and within 6 months opened the transition home to its first client. We were able to assist countless other women to secure their GED and career training to secure the kind of jobs for which they could be proud. Many of the ladies were successful in being reunited with their children and families.

As with many grassroot programs people are hesitant to support them financially and especially one that reaches out to incarcerated and/or "tainted" women. It's difficult to understand how women, the nurturer, teacher, protector, could fall into a life of crime. We all sin and fall short at some point in our lives. It is because of God's grace that we escape the shackles that beset a growing number of women in todays' society.

Habakkuk 2:3 ASV tells us, "For the vision is yet for the appointed time, and it hasteth toward the end, and shall not lie: though it tarry, wait for it; because it will surely come, it will not delay."

The vision has been modified over the years, but it is as strong as ever. We have moved beyond the ownership of bricks and mortar and are meeting people in a variety of places such as in this book and in the virtual world of social media and the classrooms of youth. As founder and director writing a monthly newsletter for more than 15 years has been challenging at best, and yet it has caused me to stretch in so many ways and when others can be blessed by what you feel and convey, one can't help but feel that they are operating in their purpose. I pray that this book has helped you to gain what you seek, remember to trust the process and trust the Processor to gain victory for yourself and family.

Bibliography

There are many literary sources referenced in this book. To each I say thank you for sharing your wisdom with us. They include the following:

Biblical references include the King James Version, King James International Version, the New King James Version, Message and Amplified Version.

Charles R. Swindoll – The Finishing Touch

Ralph Waldo Imerson

Today's Gift (Hazeldon)

National Domestic Violence Hotline

National Dating Abuse Helpline

VictimsofCrime,org

Nathan Sawaya

Gary Chapman – The 5 Love Languages

T.D. Jakes (The Potter's House)

Vocabulary,com

MentalHealth.gov

Judith Davis -Mental Health (Health,usnews.com)

Kira O – 10 Benefits of Hugging

Redskinedwizard & Burton Dewitt

DVIPIOWA.org

http:jezebel.com

NCADV.org

National Screening for Mental Health Organization

Let's Keep in Touch!

We are here for you. Visit us online at **MaeDixon.com** for lots of online resources to empower, inspire, and motivate you whenever you need it.
Subscribe at maedixon62@gmail.com for Email Newsletter and Notices of special events, to Book for Speaking Engagements, Schedule Private Counseling Sessions and to share your comments.

 facebook.com/maedixonLLC

 maedixon62

 @mdixon

*Mae Dixon is the Founder of A Will & Way, Inc., a 501 (c) 3 Non-profit organization. Net proceeds from this and other literary projects authored by Mae Dixon will be used to support its Domestic Violence programs.